Advance Praise for *Like a Tree*

"In this book, Jean Bolen expresses the essence of our deep connection to and inseparability from trees. Trees have stood by us humans always; it is the least we can do to protect and save and honour them now. Bolen's thoughts and suggestions for moving forward will, as always, help us see and feel how this might be done. This is a conversation with the Tree tribe not to be missed or dismissed."

—ALICE WALKER

"Read Jean Shinoda Bolen's *Like a Tree*, and you will never again see one without knowing it has a novel inside, that it's supporting your life, and that it's more spiritual than any church, temple, or mosque. *Like a Tree* is the rare book that not only informs, but offers a larger consciousness of life itself."

—GLORIA STEINEM

"I'll always remember the sadness I felt several years ago when I drove my little girl to her first day of the new school year and saw that the huge tree that had always welcomed us as we entered the driveway in front of the school was gone. Upon inquiring about what had happened, I was told that the tree had been removed to make way for a new sports field. I couldn't believe how sad I was or how little my sadness seemed to be shared by other people at the school. It was then that I realized what a profound shift in worldview is necessary in order for us to save the planet. I applaud everyone— including the brilliant and glorious Jean Shinoda Bolen—for helping us make the shift. Bravo, Jean. You make us feel it."

—MARIANNE WILLIAMSON

"In *Like a Tree*, Jean Bolen lovingly and simply explains to the reader why trees are our essential partners in life on Mother Earth. The book helps to unravel and integrate some of the scientific facts and spiritual values which have nurtured the development of plentiful ecosystems on our planet for many thousands of years. She also underscores the importance of today's children (especially girls) and future generations in reversing this trend, which I agree is absolutely essential."

—DONNA GOODMAN, founder and president of
Earth Child Institute

"*Like a Tree* is a terrific book. It's not only a very readable compendium of facts about various kinds of trees, but a treasury of wisdom about why we love them, how we love them, and how this love is part and parcel of life on earth. While alerting us to the pending disaster of climate change and other collective mistakes we have made through moving personal testimony, this book also gives us a good starting point for change."

—SUSAN GRIFFIN, author of *Woman and Nature: The Roaring Inside Her*

"Once again, Bolen inspires us with her wisdom, passion, and activism. *Like a Tree* is an invitation for all to see our interconnectedness and our oneness. It is simply brilliant!"

—ZAINAB SALBI, author of *Between Two Worlds* and
founder of Women for Women International

"Jean Shinoda Bolen…has come out with a most igniting, inspiring, and compassionate book that is bound to motivate thousands upon thousands of people into action in regards to the dire plight of girls, women, and trees in the world today."

—JERRY JAMPOLSKY, MD, founder of Attitudinal
Healing and Diane Cirincione, PhD, executive
director of Attitudinal Healing International

"Once again, Jean takes us to a higher level of collective activism with a timely and metaphoric message for global survival. I applaud her call to action to save the planet with a new coalition of trees, women, and 'tree people.' Count me in."

—MARILYN FOWLER, president & CEO of Women's Intercultural Network (WIN) and vice president of US Women Connect

"In *Like a Tree*, Bolen provides an original and provocative look at the relationship between trees and ourselves, and their capacity to foster not only healing, but show us the power of interdependence internally and externally. This book is a call to social and environmental action that will truly make a difference."

—ANGELES ARRIEN, PhD, cultural anthropologist and author of *The Second Half of Life: Opening the Eight Gates of Wisdom*

"In *Like a Tree*, Jean Shinoda Bolen writes that 'not enough trees, too many people' is simple arithmetic that is a prescription for disaster. She notes that what is best for the individual woman—education, contraceptives, equality, and reproductive choice—will also be best for the planet. A genuine commitment to empower women is central to a healthier, kinder, more equitable culture and one that will sustain the quality of human life."

—GLORIA FELDT, author of *No Excuses: 9 Ways Women Can Change How We Think about Power* and past president of Planned Parenthood Federation of America

"*Like a Tree* is masterful—a many-branched, mystical manifesto possessing the potential to nourish the taproots of life-enhancing cultures. Reading it will quicken the seed of your own most fulfilling and potent participation in our more-than-human world during this urgent time of immense dangers and evolutionary opportunities."

—BILL PLOTKIN, author of *Soulcraft* and *Nature and the Human Soul*

"As someone who has spent over a quarter of a century working in and out of a cathedral, I was deeply moved by this book's parallel between a redwood forest and a cathedral. Jean Shinoda Bolen touches the sacred mission of trees, women, and all life on this planet. She rings a bell that calls us to an expanded awareness and to positive action."

—Rt. Rev. WILLIAM E. SWING, seventh bishop of
the Episcopal Diocese of California and founder and
president of the United Religions Initiative

"*Like a Tree* serves as a deep and abundant well of useful facts, role models, metaphors, connections, resources, and, above all, inspiring stories about trees and women that can be drawn on to validate and bolster one's own confidence. Like a tree, this book can sustain its reader for the long haul and mightily show us the way."

—ANDY LIPKIS, founder and president of TreePeople

"*Like a Tree* is for anyone who has ever admired, felt soothed by, or loved being in a tree, under trees, or in the woods. Bolen helps us to understand that trees are our life-support system. A great read for anyone who cares about the future of people and planet!"

—NINA SIMONS, cofounder and co-CEO, Bioneers

"We shouldn't simply be alarmed by what's happening to our forests and our other fellow creatures. We should feel sick to our souls. And in this, as Jean Bolen says, women are taking the lead and showing, all over the world, that 'ordinary people' can make a difference—and that, if they don't, nobody else will. Altogether, an excellent and timely book."

—COLIN TUDGE, biologist and author of *The Tree:*
A Natural History of What Trees Are, How They Live,
and Why They Matter

Like a Tree

*How Trees, Women, and
Tree People Can Save the Planet*

by Jean Shinoda Bolen, MD

Conari Press

Cover Design: Jim Warner
Cover Photo: © Pauline H. Tesler, "Author in Monterey Cypress Tree
(*Cupressus macrocarpa*)"
Layout & Design: Maureen Forys, Happenstance Type-O-Rama

For permission requests, please contact the publisher at:
Mango Publishing Group
2850 S Douglas Road, 2nd Floor
Coral Gables, FL 33134 USA
info@mango.bz

For special orders, quantity sales, course adoptions and corporate sales, please
email the publisher at sales@mango.bz. For trade and wholesale sales, please
contact Ingram Publisher Services at customer.service@ingramcontent.com or
+1.800.509.4887.

Like a Tree: How Trees, Women, and Tree People Can Save the Planet

Library of Congress Cataloging-in-Publication Data 2020946294
ISBN: (p) 978-1-64250-406-4 (e) 978-1-64250-407-1
NAT014000, NATURE / Ecosystems & Habitats / Forests & Rainforests

Printed in the United States of America

CONTENTS

FOREWORD

by
Terry Tempest Williams

It was an early morning in December. Jean invited me to walk with her in her sacred place within the Muir Woods in Marin County, California. We were in retreat, two women, soul sisters sharing truths, telling stories, finding joy.

Our friendship is one of Spirit. I can't tell you when we met or how, only that we came into one another's lives in the deep sense through a visitation from her son, Andy, in Utah's red rock desert. Andy and I had never met. We met through the miraculous. He had died at twenty-nine from a rare disease. I learned of Andy's death from Jean. He appeared to me shortly thereafter. It was in the year 2001. It was hot, dry. I had just returned from visiting a rock covered with petroglyphs–handprints, spirals, and deer—carved by the Ancient Ones. Back home, seated on the porch, I saw him. He spoke. What Andy said will remain private between Jean and I. What it created between the two of us is a living river of sisterhood that continues to flow through us in times of drought and in times of flood. In 2019, our friendship brought us to trees.

"There are Tree People and Not Tree People," Jean said to me matter-of-factly as we crossed the wooden walkway from her front door on our way to walk among the redwoods. As she says in this vital book, "A tree person met up with Nature in childhood or as an adult, and like the four-footed ones who retreat to lick their wounds, may still heal emotional hurts by going to where the trees are."

We are going to where the trees are.

Jean then recounted the story of the beautiful Monterey pine that graced her home, rooted there long before Mill Valley's homes were built. It was a living, dignified presence that she greeted daily. Through a tragic and complicated maze of events, told in these pages, the Monterey pine was eventually slated to be killed, cut down, removed.

I shared my story of losing a tree friend, a magnificent red oak planted in Cambridge, Massachusetts, behind the Harvard Divinity School two centuries ago, before the school existed. My office looked out on this beloved "Divinity Tree" and each day I walked by, something passed between us. I would sit next to it, watch it pass through the seasons, and witness all who inhabited its mighty trunk and branches, be it squirrels, kestrels, red-tailed hawks, or ants. Like Jean's beloved Monterey pine, through a tragic and complicated maze of events, the Divinity Tree was also slated to be killed, cut down, removed after doing all we could do as a community to save its life.

There are Tree People and Not Tree People.

We both mourned the Monterey pine and the red oak, both emblematic of the millions of trees being uprooted daily by deforestation worldwide in the Amazonian rainforest, in the Congo, in the recent fires in Australia, in the slaying of old growth forests of the Pacific Northwest, and by ongoing development in California and Utah.

Thankfully, the redwoods in the Muir Woods remain.

In 1908, President Theodore Roosevelt declared 554 acres of old growth coastal redwood forests a national monument: the first ever to be created from land donated by private individuals, in this case Mr. William Kent and his wife Elizabeth Thacher Kent.

By the beginning of the twentieth century, most of the coastal redwoods in Northern California had been cut down by the logging industry. This was a bold move to protect some of the last stands of *Sequoia sempervirens*, trees that can grow up to 380 feet tall and can live for close to two thousand years. The national monument was named after the naturalist writer John Muir who worked most of his life to protect wild lands in Northern California, particularly in Yosemite, which was declared a national park in 1890.

Roosevelt, Mr. and Mrs. Kent, and John Muir were Tree People.

Jean and I arrived at the entrance to the Muir Woods very close to dawn. Once we crossed the threshold into the presence of the redwoods, we walked in silence. This is where Jean walks repeatedly for solace. I was her guest and followed respectfully behind her, wanting to honor her spiritual practice.

The woods were radiant with birdsong, the voices of thrushes and vireos; shafts of morning light falling diagonally struck individual leaves of thimbleberries turning them momentarily silver bright. Few were on the path and I couldn't help but imagine the Miwok people who inhabited this sacred grove long before the settlers and how they must have viewed these sacred towering elders we call Sequoias, how their descendants today still perform the necessary ceremonies to honor them.

The Miwok are Tree People.

At one point, Jean turned to me and invited me to step inside with her one of the hollowed trunks of a redwood that had been struck by lightning. The entrance was charred in the shape of a tall triangle flanked on either side by supporting redwoods. We were two women lodged inside a tree more than a thousand years old. I closed my eyes; Jean, now in her early eighties, held my hand. I felt my mother and grandmothers standing with us. Jean left. I stayed. This moment felt like an initiation into my own wisdom at sixty-four years of age. Who are we without our elders to show us the path forward, especially in "these liminal times" as Jean Shinoda Bolen calls them, "threshold times." The in-between times that we feel so acutely during this pandemic that has brought us to our knees.

Jean wanted to show me the historic Cathedral Grove where delegates from fifty-one countries met in San Francisco on May 19, 1945, to create and sign the United Nations Charter after World War II. The delegates convened in the Muir Woods and selected this particular grove to commemorate a vision of global peace. A plaque was dedicated to the memory of President Franklin Delano Roosevelt who had died a month short of opening the United Nations Conference on International Organization, where this inauguration occurred.

She read me the plaque: *"Here in this grove of enduring redwoods, preserved for posterity, members of the United Nations Conference on International Organization met on May 19, 1945, to honor the memory of Franklin Delano Roosevelt, thirty-first President of the United States, chief architect of the United Nations, and apostle of lasting peace for all mankind."*

Given all the work, Jean has done with the United Nations and the Commission on the Status of Women, alongside her dream of a Fifth World Conference on Women that will meet in India in 2022, this site held particular meaning. In so many ways, the vision of women's circles that Jean has been advocating for and creating with women for decades is naturally illustrated in the cycles and circles of growth exemplified within this coastal redwood ecosystem.

As the morning light deepened by the density of the woods, Jean walked ahead with a purpose. She wanted to show me her own private shrine where she meditates and communes with those she loved who have died. We had been discussing these things the night before in candlelight. She was far ahead. And then, she turned back.

"I can't find it," she said. "How strange. I've been here a thousand times."

She walked back, looking toward the stream. Walked forward again. Back. Forward. And I noted the puzzled look on her face. All at once, she saw the old path somewhat hidden by new vegetation with a recently constructed fence built with a different opening, funneling people toward a different path further away from the stream.

Access was blocked to the tree chapel Jean had come to rely on for contemplation.

I asked Jean if she wanted to step over the fence to connect with the familiar path to her shrine.

"No need," she said. "The path is inside me. The chapel is inside me, where those beloved to me also dwell." She laughed, not out of amusement, but understanding.

"The world is changing." she said. "We know change is coming. But we are always surprised when it does."

We stood in silence for a long time. Jean Shinoda Bolen misses little and as a Jungian scholar and renowned psychiatrist, she has a deep understanding of symbols and archetypes. Because of her classic book, *Goddesses in Everywoman* and her beautiful book, *Artemis: The Indomitable Spirit in Everywoman*, I made a special pilgrimage to the ancient temple of Artemis in Turkey to better understand this Goddess of Nature, Goddess of the Moon, I identified with as also one who is comfortable walking in moonlight where "her companions were the nymphs of forest, lake, and mountains." I knew Jean was beginning to comprehend something within herself that was both private and profound with her vast reservoir of intuition and knowledge, alongside her respect for synchronicity.

"Shall we go back?" she said. By now, more people were on the path coming up as we were going down. We continued to walk together quietly, talking little, but sharing much. I kept breathing in the freshness of the air, the gift of oxygen being exhaled by the redwoods, aware of the bay laurel's fragrance, the wild roses in bloom and, again, birdsong echoing in the high canopys of the big trees.

"Oh look," Jean said with enthusiasm, "A Fairy Circle!" We stopped as she explained to me what we were seeing. Before us appeared a perfect circle of young redwoods that were growing around the stump of a logged, old-growth sequoia.

"There is always the next generation," she said with her charismatic smile and laughter. "There is always the new that is seeded from that which has been destroyed."

When Jean Shinoda Bolen talks about the Millionth Circle Initiative, about the power of the circle and the women who convene around it, I think about the circles of sequoias in the Muir Woods and throughout the range of the coastal redwoods standing their ground in the shadow of destruction in the midst of a burning planet, holding hope upward in the radiance of their beings rooted in the seeds of past generations.

Tree People.

In this planetary pause where we have all been called home because of an invisible virus that is not something outside us, but inside us—both virus and human of Earth—it behooves each of us to remember and allow to take root what it means to be present with change.

Not long ago, Jean wrote to me, "The hope is that there is enough time for trees and tree people to save our beautiful planet from turning into a wasteland... We are in a period of crisis—where danger and opportunity exist side by side."

Jean Shinoda Bolen is a force of radiant joy and wisdom. *Like a Tree* is a manifesto that is evergreen: practical, visionary, and wise. Jean is an activist with great heart who has not only weathered change, but embodies an evolutionary consciousness dependent on change if we are to survive and carry on through the generations: what Native People have always known in their traditional knowledge intrinsically bound to earth, water, fire, and air—all elements rooted in the consciousness of trees. And what wisdom keepers all over the world are praying we remember.

"Another world is not only possible," Arundhati Roy writes, "she is on her way. Maybe many of us won't be here to greet her, but, on a quiet day, if I listen very carefully, I can hear her breathing."

On my walk with Jean Shinoda Bolen, I not only heard this arboreal inhale and exhale among the coastal redwoods, I felt it as the breathing space of ceremony.

PREFACE

This edition could not be timelier, as it emerges in print in the second year of the coronavirus pandemic. The destruction of one very special pine tree that had been in front of my house led me to write this book about trees ahead of its time. Now there have been massive fires over the hills of California where I live; millions of trees have gone up in flames, as well as hundreds of homes. Dry lightning not followed by rain set off hundreds of fires, and downed electrical lines did their part.

Wildfires, trees burning, smoke so thick that, for days at a time, the sky looked like a thick ominous fog and the sun appeared to be a round red orb that we could look at directly. One day the sky became an intense dull orange for the whole day. I couldn't see past the railing on my front deck. People drove slowly with their headlights on. With high winds and very little humidity, hundred of thousands of acres of trees and underbrush on hillsides and valleys were afire.

Trees are to the atmosphere in which live and breathe as the placenta is to a fetus. Trees give us the oxygen we breathe in and absorb the carbon in the carbon dioxide we breathe out, just as the placenta brought us oxygen and nourishment and took away waste while we were in the womb. The once vast forests that covered the planet have been cut down; the remaining rainforests and arboreal forests are diminishing, logged to be replaced by cash crops and to make paper, cardboard, and lumber. Meanwhile, the world's population keeps growing. The result: *not enough trees and too many people* = global warming, a disaster in the making.

In this book, I share what I learned about the marvels that trees are, and I tell about women who have been saving them. *Tree People* is my name for those of us—children, men and women—who are drawn to trees and to nature, much of which is spiritual and soul nourishing.

This edition has a new cover with photographs of Wangari Maathai, who led the Green Belt Movement of women in Kenya to plant sixteen millions trees, and Julia Butterfly Hill, who as a young woman slowed the destruction of old growth forest trees in California by living high up in one for two years, coming down only after an agreement was reached to stop logging more of this particular forest. I tell about them in this book. The other two photos are of my friend Terry Tempest Williams, an author, educator, and environmental activist who wrote the foreword to this book, and of me sitting in a tree that was on the original cover.

INTRODUCTION

The seed idea for this book began with the observation that there are "tree people," and that I am one of them. A tree person has positive feelings for individual trees and an appreciation of trees as a species. A tree person may have been a child who kept treasures in a tree, or had a sanctuary in one, or climbed up to see the wider world, a child for whom trees were places of imaginative play and retreat. A tree person is someone who may have learned about trees in summer camp or through earning a scout badge or was a child who could lose track of time in nearby woods or the backyard. A tree person met up with Nature in childhood or as an adult, and like the four-footed ones who retreat to lick their wounds, may still heal emotional hurts by going to where the trees are. A tree person understands why a young woman might spend over two years in an old growth, ancient redwood, in order to protect it from being cut down. A tree person can become a tree activist at any age.

A huge Monterey pine stood in front of the house that is now my home. I noticed it before I walked down the walk and across the entry deck to enter the house. It never occurred to me that by a vote of a homeowners association this beautiful tree that was here before any houses went up and was in its prime could be cut down because a neighbor wanted it down and could mobilize the necessary votes. In trying to save my tree, I was in many conversations and meetings, and found that there is a world of difference between tree people and "not-tree people."

I also found that there is a world of information to learn about trees, beginning with why this particular kind of tree thrives on a hillside ridge that often has a morning blanket of fog. Pine needles act as fog condensers that drip moisture down to the ground and, in effect, they water themselves. Tree people like me see the beauty of trees and may have photographed or painted them, but we may have a limited botanical knowledge of them. As I thought about writing this book, I remembered reading the classic novel *Moby-Dick,* and recalled how information about whales was interspersed throughout the narrative. I wanted to do something similar in this book, and in the process of learning about what a tree is and that they are the oldest living beings on Earth, I acquired a sense of wonder about them.

Rain forests have been called the lungs of the planet. Forests take in prodigious amounts of carbon dioxide, bind the carbon into themselves, and create oxygen, which is then released into the atmosphere we breathe. Each individual tree does this, just as each individual human, just by breathing, produces carbon dioxide, which trees use. We have a reciprocal relationship with trees. Meanwhile, the tropical rain forests and arboreal forests in North America, northern Europe, and Asia are disappearing at an accelerating rate, while the number of humans grows geometrically. Global warming is related to the increase in carbon dioxide, methane, and other gases in the atmosphere, which humans produce indirectly through what we use. The more humans there are and the fewer trees there are, the more carbon there will be in the atmosphere and the warmer it will get.

Like a Tree is a title that draws upon the use of the word "like" as simile. There are chapter headings such as "Standing *Like* a Tree" or "Sacred *Like* a Tree" that describe similarities between trees, people, and symbols. "Like" is also a verb meaning having some affection for: as in "Do you *like* this tree?" Tree people can have a range of feelings for individual trees as well as particular species. We relate to trees in ways that not-tree people never do. The polarities of contrast between a tree person and a not-tree person: Joyce Kilmer's "I think that I shall never see / A poem lovely as a tree" and the statement attributed to Ronald Reagan, "You see one tree, you've seen them all."

On the day that my Monterey pine was cut down, I was not there to see it happen. I had done all I could do, short of organizing a demonstration to save it. The tree cutters would do the deed when I was away, and with a heavy heart I anticipated the loss on my return. I was in New York City at the United Nations. For years now, I have been going to the United Nations when the Commission on the Status of Women meets in March. Parallel meetings and workshops are held by non-governmental organizations concerned with protecting and empowering women and girls and with women's rights. The exercise of dominion over women and girls can take many terrible forms: trafficking, female genital mutilation, stoning women, honor-killings, or selling daughters to settle a debt. Closer to home, women and girls are dominated and demeaned through domestic violence, rape, and the sexual abuse of children. Physically and psychologically, when a girl or woman is treated as property, she is "Like a Tree"—or the dog or horse that can be valued, loved, and treated well or worked, beaten, and sold. These are behaviors and patterns rooted in raising boys to identify with the aggressor and raising girls to learn powerlessness. These are distortions of natural growth. A tree that receives what it needs of sun and rain, healthy soil for its roots, and room to grow becomes a healthy mature tree and a fine specimen. When conditions stunt growth, the result is usually a still-recognizable version of a particular kind of tree. In human beings, unless signs of malnutrition or abuse are visible to the eye, the stunted growth that results from withholding love, nutrition, medical attention, education, and human rights usually manifests as psychological, intellectual, and spiritual stunting, in *all* concerned.

The tree is a powerful symbol. Trees appear in many creation stories, such as the World Ash or the Garden of Eden. Religions, especially the Druids, have revered trees. Buddha was enlightened sitting under a Bodhi tree. Christmas is celebrated by decorating Christmas trees. There are sacred trees throughout the world. "Family tree" has a symbolic connection to the theme of immortality. Myths and symbols are the carriers of meaning. In them, a situation is presented metaphorically in a language of image, emotion, and symbol. Because human beings share a collective unconscious (C. G. Jung's psychological explanation) or the *Homo sapiens* morphic field (Rupert Sheldrake's biological explanation), a symbol comes from and resonates with the deeper layers of the human psyche.

Like a Tree circles around the subject of tree: the result is a series of views, from many different perspectives. Mythology and archetypal psychology are sources of information about the symbolic meaning of the tree. Botany and biology classify and describe. To learn about trees is to appreciate them as a species. Beliefs about sacred trees and symbols of them have been part of many religions, and turned trees into casualties of religious conflicts. The unintended consequences of cutting down all the trees on Easter Island were disastrous, with applicable parallels to the fate of the planet. In Kenya, the Green Belt Movement engaged rural women to plant trees. When this became known through honoring the founder, Wangari Maathai, thirty million trees had been planted and, in 2004, she became the first African woman to be awarded the Nobel Peace Prize.

As I went deeper and deeper into the subject of trees, I entered a complex and diverse forest of knowledge, from archeological to mystical. I learned that we wouldn't be here at all—we, the mammals and humans on this planet—if not for trees. Whether huge forests or a single specimen that is one of the oldest living things on Earth, trees continue to be cut down by corporations or individuals motivated by greed or poverty, who are ignorant of or indifferent to the consequences or meaning of what they do. I learned that reforestation was the difference between cultures that stayed in place and thrived, and those that cut down the trees and did not: these are very applicable object lessons for humanity now. It's possible to learn from past history and see what will befall us or how trees may save us.

I've grasped a parallel learning from going to the United Nations when the Commission on the Status of Women meets. Women and girls are a resource. Educate a girl, and she will marry later, have fewer, healthier children, and almost all her earnings will benefit her family. With micro-credit loans, women start their own small businesses. When there are enough women in high enough positions, such as in Liberia and Rwanda, the previous culture of corruption and violence disappears. Priorities shift to safety, education, and health. With peace, the economy grows. A convincing case can be made that participation by women is the missing key element in finding solutions for the financial, environmental, and military problems that underlie the instability of our world and the questions of survival or sustainability. Valuing girls is like valuing trees. It's good for them and for the planet.

There is a proliferation of grassroots activism. Nongovernmental organizations (NGOs) have been cropping up all over the world, numbering in the millions, including in China and Russia as well as Africa. Women grow small businesses into larger ones, and have been creating NGOs (80 percent are created by women) with the potential to change collective thinking. Ideas now can spread like a virus, which overcomes resistance to become commonplace. For a tree person who reads my words, whose awareness and concern have not yet extended beyond caring about particular trees, my intention is to take your consciousness deeper, as mine has gone, to involve your heart, mind, and imagination as the first step toward participation in saving trees and girls.

All that was left of my Monterey pine when I came home was the substantial stump; it was broad, irregularly shaped, beautiful in a way, still raw from the cutting and oozing sap. There was also an empty space against the sky where it once towered over my walk.

During the week I was away, when my tree was cut down, I talked to Gloria Steinem about my unsucessful saga to save my tree. She said, "Remember Jean, you are a writer and a writer can have the last word." Many trees are cut down to make paper, which is the usual way a tree can become a book. My tree lives on through the words and spirit in this book.

1
STANDING LIKE A TREE

I often walk among the ancient soaring coast redwood trees in Muir Woods, the national park close to where I live in California. I have to crane my neck to look up at them, much like a toddler who would otherwise just see kneecaps or legs of adults. Though in proportion to the height of these trees, I'm not even at toenail level. These tall conifers are descendants of the green leafy tree ferns and first trees, without which Earth would not have breathable air, soil, or rainwater. As the BBC documentary *Planet Earth* succinctly said of our biological relationship to trees, "If they didn't live here, neither would we." My study of trees began with looking up specific information about the Monterey pine (*Pinus radiata*), which is how I learned why it had been particularly suited to where I live. About the same time, I had begun a practice of taking early morning walks in Muir Woods. Both led me metaphorically deeper into the trees.

My wonder of trees keeps growing as I learn more about what they are and do. It has also been learning for the sake of it. Trees seem so ordinary and familiar and unmoving: they just stand wherever they took root and, until we know better, don't seem to be doing anything much. Those with the oldest lineage are members of the conifer family. The conifers do nothing showy—no autumn colors, spring blossoms, or glorious fruit—but when they are noticed and we understand how wonderful they are, a depth and poetic appreciation can result. Out of their wonder and love of the trees they study, naturalists have written about them with poetic sensibility. John Muir, America's most famous and influential naturalist, for example, described a juniper as "a sturdy storm-enduring mountaineer of a tree, living on sunshine and snow, maintaining tough health on his diet for perhaps more than a thousand years" (Muir, *My First Summer in the Sierra*, 1911, p. 146). Muir's ability to describe what he saw in the high Sierras and Yosemite Valley, to write of the awe he felt in the presence of the ancient redwoods, and to influence others had a significant role in preserving them, including Muir Woods.

In *The Tree*, a comprehensive book on the subject, the English author and naturalist Colin Tudge compares the building of a beautiful cathedral with how a tree grows, a comparison in which the tree comes out ahead:

> [A] cathedral or a mosque is built; it does not grow. Until it is complete it is useless, and probably unstable. It must be held up by scaffold. When it is finished it remains as it was made for as long as it lasts—or until some later architect designs it afresh, and rebuilds. A tree, by contrast, may grow to be tall as a church and yet must be fully functional from the moment it germinates. It must fashion and refashion itself as it grows, for as it increases

in size so the stresses alter—the tension and compression on each part. To achieve hugeness and yet be self-building—no scaffold or outside agencies required—and to operate for good measure as an independent living creature through all phases of growth is beyond anything that human engineers have achieved. (2006, p. 75)

What Exactly Is a Tree?

Trees are *arboreal perennials:* they have a columnar woody stem with branches growing from it. The height varies according to the specific species, environment, and various other factors, though normally they reach a height of twenty feet (six meters) or more. The shape and general development of a tree are so characteristic that the category also includes species of lesser size, such as dwarf trees.

In the delightful way that the English have with words, Colin Tudge begins his answer with what every child knows: "A tree is a big plant with a stick up the middle" (*The Tree,* p. 3) and proceeds to be eloquent and scientific, a small part of which I paraphrase and pass on here.

Some two to three billion years ago, a layer of vegetation grew upon barren rocks—a slime perhaps no thicker than a coat of paint, made of bacteria, molds, mosses, lichens, algae, and fungi. Chlorophyll in algae made the slime greenish and photosynthesis possible: the energy from sunlight (photons) was used to make sugars and stored by algae. This was the significant first step. Stalks formed slowly, slowly over many, many millions of years, grew from nubbin to matchstick to become ferns that proliferated and grew to enormous size in the Carboniferous period, which began about 350 million years ago. This was a time when giant forests of huge tree ferns covered the Earth. These tree ferns removed prodigious amounts of carbons from poisonous gases, storing it in their leaves and stalks. After millions of more years went by and layer upon layer fell into decay, pressure and time transformed these vast fern forests into coal. Removing carbon dioxide and releasing oxygen, these giant tree fern forests made the air breathable. They also made it possible for more sunlight to reach the surface of the Earth through the clearer air.

The fern forests became the womb and the nursery of the first trees. As John Stewart Collis, another English author phrased it, "In these glades was matured the idea of not falling down" (Collis, *The Triumph of the Tree*, 1954, p. 10). The ferns rose and fell, over and over again, producing stalks and branches that grew eventually to be the size of trees. In their midst, some 290 million years ago, a more energy-efficient form of plant life, which had woody trunks and branches, appeared. Wood tree trunks are structurally stronger than stalks, and they have roots that anchor the tree in the ground. Tree trunks provide a two-way conduit of water and nutrients from roots to leaves, and from leaves to the whole tree. As a tree grows above the ground, its root structure grows also. In good, deep soil, some species of trees can have as large a circulatory root system below ground as the visible branches and leaves.

The root system of trees continues to have a key role in transforming rock into soil. This process began when the planet was lifeless rock, with a thin layer of algae, mold, lichen, and fungi. Soil is made from rock that disintegrates into dust and releases minerals, plus decaying organic matter, oxygen, and water. Trees draw from and contribute to making more soil. Their roots break up and aerate rock and hard clay. Dropping leaves provide organic matter. Their leaves release water vapor and oxygen into the atmosphere, drip water into the ground below, and provide shade that prevents evaporation. Trees create the conditions for ground-covering plants to grow under them. Tree roots hold the soil down, preventing runoff after rain and keeping strong winds from carrying it away. Trees create watersheds, the source of water to feed streams and rivers. When huge areas of forests are clear-cut for timber or burned down to raise cattle, the ecological systems supported by trees—from roots to leafy canopies—are also destroyed, affecting all forms of life that once thrived there, as well as the quality of the air, soil, and water in the immediate area and far downstream.

Every large tree has an ecosystem of its own, a sphere of influence in its immediate environment. I began to think about this after my Monterey pine was cut down. There were observable consequences, beyond its absence. The resident squirrel got displaced. More direct sun instead of partial sun and shade changed what would thrive in the half dozen terra-cotta planters that I planted with annuals. Direct sun in spring and fall, morning fog in the summer had been ideal for the bright, colorful impatiens that I had planted for years, exchanging them for cyclamen as autumn approached. The tree had also sheltered many plants from the wind, which I next discovered. For the first time, in the absence of shade, I planted sun-loving petunias, which initially grew very fast and had to be watered often. Then came the summer fog, and the petunias became immediately pathetic, the blooms overnight becoming limp and mildewed. A slow-growing vine went into overdrive, sending out waving tendrils by the foot that now needed to be cut back often, before they could cover or strangle nearby rhododendrons. Now unprotected from the direct sun, rhododendron and camellia leaves became sunburnt in unusually hot weather. The side of the hill on which this particular tree had thrived for forty or so years has very poor soil; the dirt is mainly gravel and sand and very hard. Yet the ground cover and established shade-loving flowering plants and a maple tree did well, with virtually no watering. The pine needles had been a water-dripping system. Not just for itself, but also for its tree neighbors. So much so that when I went out to get the morning newspapers, the walk beneath its branches often looked as if it had rained during the night. The pine tree had been the center of an ecologically sustainable little island, which now requires watering.

Invisible to me was the ecosystem underground. Trees are part of a mutually beneficial community in all directions. Trees are a habitat for the plants, insects, birds, and animals in their vicinity, but an even closer bond is formed with the fungi and bacteria that are intimately connected to the metabolism of the tree. They eat the sugars that the tree makes and bind the hydrogen that the tree needs. Bill Mollison, the originator of permaculture, a sustainable ecological design inspired by observing rain forests, described how bacterial colonies on the leaves of trees are carried aloft by the wind high into the clouds, where ice crystals form around them, and as they get heavier and fall, they seed the clouds and cause rain to fall on the trees. The rain that falls through the tree canopy is now rain-bath water, a rich nutrient soup that washes off the minerals that were left on the leaves by evaporation, providing these nutrients for the ground cover, the little plants under the trees, and soaking into the soil, from which it will be pulled through the roots, the ends of which are covered by bacteria that are a two-way selective filter, and up the xylem of the tree to the leaves. Forests of trees keep the rain going, which is why all huge forests, whether in the tropics or on the northernmost edge of the continents, are rain forests.

Two Kinds of Trees

My tree was a conifer (conifer means "cone-bearing"), in the tree family lineage that began 290 million years ago. Conifers are familiar trees, known to us as firs, spruces, pines, cedars, redwoods, cypress, podocarps, yews, and junipers. They originated in and continue to survive in poor soil, with extremes of weather from tropical to desert, to almost arctic. Among the conifers in California are coast redwoods, the tallest trees in the world, and the bristlecone pines, which are the oldest. They comprise the vast boreal forests in Alaska, Canada, Scandinavia, Russia, and Siberia. They thrive in places where conditions are difficult, including in areas where fires are common. They are survivors and pioneers—trees that move into devastated areas and grow where other trees do not.

The conifers are one of the two large tree categories that make up 99 percent of all trees: trees without flowers (conifers) and trees with flowers (the angiosperms). Angiosperms differ from conifers in their sexuality. The female ovule is completely enclosed within the ovary, and the male gamete must be carried to it via pollen tubes. Uniquely, angiosperms practice double fertilization. This is a very brief summation; left out are definitions and explanations, the various means of union and procreation, and how this contrasts with conifers. Suffice it to note that the obstetrics and gynecology of the two categories differ. The angiosperms are a huge universe of flowering plants (300,000 species), among which there are trees. The surmise is that flowering trees with woody trunks evolved from flowering plants, with missing links. Also not known are when, where, and how angiosperms originated.

Broadleaf trees are angiosperms: they include acacia, maple, elder, baobab, alder, aralia, birch, hickory, hawthorn, laurel, eucalyptus (gum), linden, olive, beech, banyan, fig, sycamore, ash, locust, mulberry, plane, coffee, holly, poplar, aspen, oak, willow, pepper, elm, and many others. Fruit trees, nut-bearing trees, and flowering trees are also angiosperms. There are about fifty times more species of flowering trees than of conifers. They usually grow where the soil is good or adequate, in temperate zones where the weather has predictable seasons, or in the vast tropical forests of the Amazon, central Africa, or Indonesia.

Tropical Rain Forests and Boreal Rain Forests

Both tropical rain forests and boreal forests are being destroyed at an alarming rate by humans for economic reasons. In an article in *National Geographic* (Wallace, "Last of the Amazon," January 2007), Scott Wallace began with the sentence: "In the time it takes to read this article, an area of Brazil's rain forest larger than 200 football fields will have been destroyed." Industrial-scale soybean producers are joining loggers and cattle ranchers in the land grab. Roads are cut through the forest to make valuable hardwood trees more accessible and transportable. In the Amazon, there are more than 105,000 miles of these roads, almost all made illegally, which then are used by squatters, farmers, and ranchers who clear the land by burning off the underbrush and trees that remain.

As indigenous people intuitively grasp, the benefits the Amazon provides are of incalculable worth: water cycling (the forest produces not only half its own rainfall, but also much of the rain south of the Amazon and east of the Andes), carbon sequestering (by holding and absorbing carbon dioxide, the forest mitigates global warming and cleanses the atmosphere), and maintenance of an unmatched panoply of life. But there haven't been profits in keeping the forest. Money is made by logging and by cutting it down for grazing and farming, not by leaving it standing.

Twenty percent or more of the Amazon rain forest has been cut down so far. When another 20 percent is destroyed, scientific expectations are that the forest's ecology will unravel. This would reduce the amount of rainfall that the forest produces through the moisture the trees release into the atmosphere. To this, add global warming: remaining trees then dry out, leading to droughts and susceptibility to fire. Amazon forest fires burned unchecked for months during the record drought of 2005–2006, followed in 2007 by the worst rain-forest fire in history. Smoke releases tons of carbon dioxide and other pollutants into the air, directly raising the ambient temperature, and further contributing to global warming by the production of more greenhouse gases. The deforestation story is the same in Indonesia, the country with the largest tropical forest in Southeast Asia, which replenishes fresh water and has a key role in weather and climate.

Whether my concern is about one tree or forests, one person or humanity, I learn what I need in order to grasp a situation that affects a species or a class of people (children, women, race, or religion) by paying attention to an individual that is representative. I want to see the forest *and* the trees, a metaphor that became literal. I learned from my Monterey pine that pine needles condense fog into lots of dripping water. Next I learned from others that trees also send water upward from groundwater; they transpire it from roots through leaves. Colin Tudge wrote that a big tree can transpire 500 liters (528 quarts) in a day.

In *Tree: A Life Story,* David Suzuki and Wayne Grady explained how one tree adds to the big picture: "A single tree in the Amazon rain forest lifts hundreds of liters of water every day. The rain forest behaves like a green ocean, transpiring water that rains upward, as though gravity were reversed. These transpired mists then flow across the continent in great rivers of vapor. The water condenses, falls as rain, and is pulled back up again through the trees. It rises and falls on its westward migration an average of six times before finally hitting the physical barrier of the Andes mountains and flowing back across the continent as the mightiest river of Earth" (2004, p. 68). This particular description captured my imagination and thereby my understanding.

The North American continent has its own vast, endangered boreal forests of conifers. In the waiting room of my optometrist, I picked up a six-month-old copy of *Audubon* just after I decided to write *Like a Tree*. In it, journalist T. Edward Pickens described Canada's boreal forest as "an emerald halo of woodlands, wetlands, and rivers that mantles North America. This is the greatest wilderness on the continent, a 1.3 billion-acre forest stretching from Newfoundland all the way to the Yukon. The Canadian boreal holds a quarter of the world's forests and most of its unfrozen freshwater, and sequesters 1.3 trillion metric tons of carbon" ("Paper Chase," January–February 2009). More than three hundred species of birds breed there, and as many as five billion individual birds fly south from the boreal each autumn. These trees are being clear-cut to make paper, for books, catalogs, paper towels, and toilet paper. There are clear-cut areas measured in square miles. In an issue of *National Geographic* (June 2002), I learned that boreal forests have more wetlands than anywhere else in the world. Those in Russia and Canada each contain an estimated one million to two million lakes and ponds.

Saving Rain Forests: Greenpeace's Successes

The conifers are the trees I have most bonded with, and there is a geographic affinity between California and the North American boreal conifer forests that draws me to their plight. How many pine trees are cut down is a market supply and demand decision. Whether it is done with consideration for watersheds, habitats for wildlife, or generations to come (indigenous North American tribal wisdom considered the effect of their actions on the next seven generations) is a corporate decision made by people, who do so either because they are wise or to ward off negative publicity, which would be bad for business.

Greenpeace waged a successful five-year "Kleercut" campaign to demand that Kimberly-Clark, the company that makes Kleenex, Scott, and Cottonelle paper products stop destroying ancient boreal forest trees. In August 2009, as a result of public pressure, Kimberly-Clark announced that it set a goal of obtaining 100 percent of the wood fiber used in its products from environmentally responsible sources. By 2011, Kimberly-Clark promised that 40 percent of its North American fiber will be either recycled or certified by the Forest Stewardship Council (an independent, non-governmental, nonprofit global organization that certifies and labels lumber from responsibly managed forests).

In June 2009, Greenpeace published the report "Slaughtering the Amazon," which traced cattle products (leather and beef) used in top brand running shoes, designer handbags, clothes, and fast food directly back to their origin, to ranches in the Amazon. The Brazilian cattle industry accounts for roughly 80 percent of Amazon deforestation and 14 percent of the world's annual forest loss. Greenpeace called for an immediate moratorium on further Amazon deforestation and named the companies that may be unwittingly contributing to this (and human rights abuses) through their raw material purchases. The leading global brands named were Adidas/Reebok, Nike, Carrefour, Eurostar, Unilever, Johnson & Johnson, Toyota, Honda, Gucci, Louis Vuitton, Prada, IKEA, Kraft, Tesco, and Wal-Mart.

One week after the report was published, Brazil's largest supermarket chains, including Wal-Mart and Carrefour, announced that they would be suspending their contracts with suppliers found to be involved in Amazon deforestation and would develop guidelines to ensure that cattle products were not from illegally cleared Amazon lands. The Brazilian government also responded. A federal prosecutor filed a billion-dollar suit against the cattle industry for environmental damage. Firms that sell this tainted beef may now be fined 500 *reals* ($260) per kilo (2.2 pounds).

There are activists who volunteer to be on the frontlines in their efforts to stop the clear-cutting and killing of endangered species. Success at the site means they interfered and stopped the destruction, often in spite of physical dangers from men whose livelihood or profits are interfered with. Success overall, such as this Greenpeace example in the Amazon, involved combining on-site activism with the skills and connections of activists who can get media attention and government action. This may turn out to be just a holding action that warded off the forces of greed or need for a time, and just in this one place. Or, in my more optimistic overview, this is a holding action (and there are others) that spares trees until environmentalism and saving trees rather than cutting them down becomes profitable.

As awareness of global warming increases, more tourists than ever are opting for eco-friendly holidays, which is one way saving trees and profitability may be coming together. In an October 2010 announcement, Achim Steiner, UN Under-Secretary General and United Nations Environment Programme (UNEP) Executive Director, said: "National parks and protected areas represent one key and successful response to conserving and managing this planet's nature-based assets. And in a way that can generate revenues and livelihoods for local communities. Indeed, by some estimates, $1-$2 billion of global tourism is linked to the world's network of around 150,000 protected sites." Protected sites are included under ecotourism, which takes 77 billion of the global tourism market and is growing (UNEP online).

Activism with Heart

As I learn about trees and what is happening to them, other concerns and thoughts come together: trees, global warming, effects on the soil and on animal life and on the most vulnerable people on the planet (impoverished women and children—especially girl children), as a result of corporate emphasis on short-term bottom lines, and my own collusion through what I eat, buy, and do. I come to a mental discomfort zone in myself that is familiar. With consciousness comes choice, with choice comes responsibility to do something. There is *so* much to do, so many causes and appeals. Just as the seed for this book was the destruction of one tree that was special to me, ripples of thought associations result from what I learn about what I could do, what others I know are doing, and how doing something rather than nothing does feel better. Also, whatever any of us does, if it comes from the heart and, I'd add, from a depth of feeling for what needs help and therefore from who we are, then what we do and how much is the next right action for us.

In 2006, Rebecca Hosking was horrified at seeing hundreds of bird carcasses dead from plastic bags lodged in their stomachs, went to her hometown of Modbury, England, and persuaded all of its forty-three shopkeepers to agree to a plastic-bag ban (Adams, "Rebecca Hosking: Banning Plastic Bags," *Time*, 2009, p. 52). One appalled and compassionate woman led the way; by 2009, eighty other towns in the United Kingdom had followed suit. In 2007, San Francisco Supervisor

Ross Mirkarimi's proposal banning plastic bags and requiring recyclable or compostable sacks passed to make San Francisco the first city in the United States to do so. Where I live, the grocery checkout line becomes a moment of choice: paper or plastic? (Trees or birds?) My solution, a large colorful and reusable bag that proclaims: "I used to be a plastic bottle."

Ever since I wrote *Urgent Message from Mother: Gather the Women, Save the World*, I've been a message carrier out in the world, saying, "Mother Wants You!" But consistent with the individuation work I do as a Jungian analyst, I speak of how important it is to take on what *you* recognize as being your particular *assignment*, and not something others say you ought to do. I think that when an assignment comes along with your name on it, you can recognize it by your answers to three questions that only you can answer: *"Is this meaningful?"* Every good cause is meaningful, but is this one meaningful to you? *"Will it be fun?"* Not to underestimate that it will be work, may take courage, and may mark you as weird, but to make the point: will you be in good company, are these people with whom you can laugh and cry, work through difficulties, and stand shoulder to shoulder? Fun also has to do with tapping into your creativity and using who you are for a cause close to your heart. And last, *"Is it motivated by love?"* Love of what or whom you care about and want to help or save generates energy; success is measured by your heart in the small stories as well as in achieving goals.

You may not feel a strong, inaudible call to your activist soul when the desire to make a difference and ways to do so grows slowly, one step at a time. Many activists began as volunteers, recruited from the sidelines. When help was needed, they showed up. Activism often begins by doing one thing, and then the next right thing. It may begin with emails that raise your hackles or your consciousness, or calls to your compassionate heart. The first active step may be the petitions you sign and the donations you make. It may lead to going to meetings or a conference. One thing leads to another and you find your assignment. However you get there, once you recognize and commit to your assignment, it will likely take more than you expected and give more in return.

The Naturalist Who Became a Writer-Activist

I came across Joan Dunning, who exemplifies just this, when a title in the used book section at my local bookstore, Book Passage, caught my eye: *From the Redwood Forest: Ancient Trees and the Bottom Line: A Headwaters Journey*, which she wrote. Joan was asked by a friend, "Will you just come to a meeting?" She said yes simply to get her friend to stop nagging, thinking it would also be token support for her local ecosystem. Joan was a naturalist who studied birds and was asked to read from a chapter she had written on the marbled murrelet, an unusual, robin-sized seabird, which should be a ground nester like the rest of its family but instead makes its nest in the tallest living things on Earth. High in redwood forests, the marbled murrelet incubates one glass-green egg in a depression in a bed of thick lichens.

As Joan read, she became aware of all the emotion behind the observant naturalist that she is. The assignment she took on was this book, written for "the millions of parents who take care of every aspect of their children's lives but one: whether the Earth itself will survive." Her guides were the young people she met, mostly in their twenties. A young man who spent nights and days in a small hammock suspended high above the ground attached to the trunk of one of these redwoods was one of her teachers. He gave a firsthand description of what he witnessed as these ancient trees are felled, beginning with the creation of the fall-bed to cushion the fall so the massive tree won't splinter, to how just before it falls, it begins to vibrate, tremble, and then shake as if it were still alive, then, slowly at first, begins to lean. Others have said that they sometimes hear a sound like a shrieking cry at the point that a great tree starts to fall.

When she looks up at old growth trees that are still standing, Joan thinks about him and what he willingly did. I like how she described the young activists whose efforts would be only partially successful: "They stand . . . with the majesty of old-growth redwoods . . . straight and tall like the few stands of old growth that still remain" (*From the Redwood Forest,* 1998, p. 4).

The Tree Sitter and the Passerby

On Vancouver Island, in June 2010, Hilary Huntley, a young Canadian artist, suddenly became a tree activist when she learned that three majestic Garry oaks (*Quercus garryana*) were to be cut down for a sports field and took immediate personal action. She climbed into one of them, determined to thwart the tree cutters, and became the center of a spontaneous community effort to save them. A day after Hilary climbed into her perch, Clare Peterson was taking a morning walk on a trail nearby when she heard a loud voice calling "Hello!" Clare looked around, didn't see anyone, but responded with a hello right back. The voice said, "Over here!" which took her to the foot of the giant Garry oak and to Hilary, who said, "Did you know that they are planning to cut down this tree on Tuesday morning? They will have to take me with it. I'm staying right here and am not moving."

Clare told me that as she walked away, she asked herself, "Why would I get involved? What could I do?" And as she wondered, "What would I sit up in a tree for?" she suddenly heard herself say, "I must support any woman who will sit in a tree for what she believes." Energized now, she tapped into her organizing abilities, and networks that were already in place went into action. A tree vigil formed. Everyone did her bit, from phoning powers that be and the baseball clubs, to bombarding city council members with emails and phone calls, to alerting local media that covered the story. A ten-year-old girl was told by her mother to skip school to be with the tree people and learn something. Four days later, the trees were saved. Hilary stayed in the tree until the mayor called her on her cell phone saying the trees would be preserved. "Great!" she said. "Once I have it in writing, I will get down." The official document was delivered within an hour. And, since a phone tree had been organized, "The trees are saved!" went out all over the valley, very quickly.

After it was over and Hilary came down from the tree, Clare, who is a Millionth Circle convener who with Anne Caldwell and others organized Gather the Women–Canada, wrote, "One of the most valuable things I saw was that everyone who gets involved and is present to the actual event notices how each person holds a piece of the solution. Passion brings people out and that passion ensures that each particular skill contributes to the resolution . . . rather like Circle Principles!"

Once the people in the town of Duncan became informed about plans to cut down these Garry oaks—which they did because of Hilary, Clare, and many others—people who learned and cared about saving the trees swung into action; this was an intergenerational effort. As a consequence, there is more community awareness about trees with the hope of a tree-preservation bylaw becoming adopted. In Canada, Garry oaks grow only in southeastern Vancouver Island and the Gulf Islands, with some isolated trees elsewhere. The Garry oak was named by botanist and explorer David Douglas for Nicholas Garry of the Hudson's Bay Company, who helped him during his travels.

Tree preservation consciousness is needed to save trees, especially when new owners purchase property with the intent to clear and build, with no regard for the old and beautiful trees that are there. Soon after I heard from Clare, for example, I learned from Patricia Damery, a Jungian analyst in Napa Valley, California, that new owners might clear a hilltop area with a ring of huge valley oaks in a large circle and other landmarks to plant vineyards. This land has been used for rituals and is sacred space for her and quite possibly was used as such when indigenous tribes lived there. The challenge is to approach owners in the same spirit as did the tree people in Canada, without rage or blame, and mobilize the concern of the community for its special trees, possibly with the added American incentive that if land and trees such as these are donated to a land trust, there can be tax benefits. Intergenerational activism may be required to protect the trees while agreements to save them can be worked out. Tree sitting and consequent media attention are done by young adult activists who are aware that once trees are cut down, the conversation is over, while mature, established citizen-taxpayer tree people are the ones that have political influence, especially locally, which is where tree issues are settled.

The Nature Speaks Project

Linda Milks became a tree activist after she received what she calls her mission in life as a communication from trees that she took to heart. She is the founder of the Nature Speaks Project. On a beautiful, sunny day in 1999, she was enjoying a drive on winding roads through the trees and hills in Marin County, north of San Francisco, when "I began to notice an organized thought form come into my awareness." It was an unusual experience for her. When it persisted, she pulled over to the side of the road to focus on the specific, telepathic communication she was receiving. She says, "I simply knew this was coming from Trees. My experience was one of listening to something coming from outside of myself and not a thought coming from within. I had no doubt that Tree consciousness was 'speaking.' They wanted a bridge of understanding between trees and humans." At the time, Linda felt the message was specifically for her, but since then, she has come to believe that it was more like an all-points bulletin, and she was one of the humans who responded. She says that at that moment, she knew that she would answer the call and that her own growth would be tied directly to this work.

This is inner knowledge, or *gnosis*—the certainty that people feel when they respond from deep recognition or *know* the significance of the choice they are making, while not knowing where it will lead and that others are likely not to understand. Yet for those with such certainty and courage to trust, the promise is that this is an authentic and meaningful choice, chosen by soul rather than ego. So the Nature Speaks Project began with Linda's idea that she would interview people who could speak with trees to record their stories.

One of the stories in the website collection (Nature Speaks Project) is Linda's own: When she was nine and lived in Lake Jackson, Texas, she took an axe to cut down a small tree. The trunk was probably about six inches in diameter, the tree ten to twelve feet tall. She approached the tree feeling powerful and excited. Then she swung the ax and made a cut into the tree. Something felt wrong; she felt she was hurting someone and shouldn't be doing this. Her reaction didn't feel rational, so she made a second cut, and at that point, she received a telepathic communication, the tone of which was "that of a wise, patient, and compassionate grandfather and it consisted mainly of questions." Such ones as she remembers had to do with why she wanted to cut down the tree, didn't she realize it was a living being, other trees and animals liked having this tree here, why would she want to hurt the tree and take its life away? She went back to the house to ask her mother about trees and if they could feel, and was told, "No, trees don't feel anything. You can cut it down if you want to." In Linda's own experience, however, she knew that her mother was wrong and that she had hurt a living, feeling being. This was her only childhood recollection of communications from trees. Forty years passed before she pulled over to the side of the road in Marin, and listened to what the Trees had to say to her.

Often significant memories of non-ordinary reality or active imagination that many people had as children fade, are forgotten, or if the child spoke of them and was made to feel ashamed, the memory becomes associated with pain and is suppressed. It is this very facility—to be psychic, mystic, attuned to energy, or transmissions of feelings or sensations, sometimes images, or intuitive impressions—that can connect adults with Nature and their own authentic nature, at a time when the fate of the planet depends on humans feeling these connections.

Still-Standing Ancient Trees

The coast redwoods in Muir Woods (*Sequoia sempervirens*) are conifers, one of the three surviving redwood species left on Earth in small pockets in isolated areas. At one time, there were two million acres of virgin coast redwood forests; now a little more than 3 percent of the original forest remains safe from loggers in state parks and one national park. Efforts to save these old growth trees on privately held land has been an ongoing struggle, beginning with John Muir, taken up by Save the Redwoods League, Earth First!, and other organizations and individuals. ("Old growth" forests are where there are no signs of past or present human activity.) The world's tallest tree is a coast redwood. The title is currently held by Stratosphere Giant at 368.6 feet in Humboldt State Park, edging out the longtime titleholder Tall Tree in Redwood National Park, which in 1990 was estimated to be over 1,500 years old and 368 feet (112 meters) tall. Twenty-six redwoods over 360 feet tall have been found, eighty-six over 350 feet. These coast redwoods are the tallest living things on Earth.

Their cousins are the giant redwoods (*Sequoiadendron giganteum*) found on the western slope of the Sierra Nevada

Mountains in California. General Sherman, a giant redwood growing in the Sequoia National Park, is the largest living thing on Earth, with an estimated age of 2,700 years, and an estimated weight of 2.7 million pounds (1.2 million kilograms). Their only other living relative is the dawn redwood, which grows in a remote area of the Hubei province in China.

These trees are ancient tree beings and great works of Nature's art. To a tree person, cutting them down for lumber would be like pulverizing Michelangelo's statues of David or the Pieta to make marble tiles, or bulldozing the acropolis in Athens as a site for a hotel.

Trees are the oldest living things on Earth. Among the bristlecone pines growing on a barren mountainside in eastern California's White Mountains, there is a 4,841-year-old (as of 2010) bristlecone (*Pinus longaeva*) named Methuselah, after the longest-lived patriarch in the biblical book of Genesis (said to have lived 969 years). Methuselah lives in a grove with others that are over four thousand years old. These trees began their lives before the great pyramids of Egypt were built. They grow on steep, rocky slopes at elevations between 9,000 feet and 11,500 feet (2,700–3,500 meters). Half the year, the temperature is below freezing, with deep snowfalls and ferocious winds. The harsh environment and the bristlecones' response to it have enabled them to reach their great age. That they don't have humans in their vicinity is one saving grace, and they are protected and in a national park, which makes their survival much more likely.

The 2009 documentary *The National Parks: America's Best Idea* by Ken Burns is a twelve-hour series that tells the story of each park as well as shows them to us. Meant to be reserved for the people for all time, national parks came into being through the fierce love that influential and often very wealthy men had for the beauty and splendor of wilderness places. Ancient forests of giant sequoias and towering redwoods as well as the bristlecone pines are now within America's national parks.

Anna Lewington and Edward Parker open their book *Ancient Trees: Trees That Live for a Thousand Years* with this quote from John Muir: "Among all the varied productions with which Nature has adorned the surface of the earth, none awakens our sympathies, or interests our imagination so powerfully as those venerable trees which seem to have stood the lapse of ages, silent witnesses of the successive generations of man, to whose destiny they bear so touching a resemblance, alike in their budding, their prime and their decay." The authors initially set out on a journey of discovery hoping to include some twenty-four species of trees that live over a thousand years. Their list rose to a hundred and the list is still growing. They comment that some of the world's oldest and most impressive inhabitants have already begun their fourth, fifth, sixth, or even seventh millennium. They report that a carbon-dated small-leaved lime tree (*Tilia cordata*) in a woodland in the west of England has already celebrated its six-thousandth birthday, and a common yew (*Taxus baccata*) in Fortingall, Scotland, could be nine thousand years old.

When I came home to find my huge beautiful Monterey pine tree was now an impressive stump, one question that could now be answered was its/her age: forty-two years old. As just about everyone knows, the age of a tree can be determined once it is cut down, by the number of its concentric growth rings. It is part of American tree lore, because this is so for trees that grow seasonally in temperate zones. In good years, the growth rings are broad; in bad growing years, such as a drought year, the rings are close together.

Tree Anatomy and Physiology

What are tree rings, anyway? The question led me to learn about the nutrient transport system inside of trees. Water travels upward through the trunk from its underground roots. A large root called the taproot grows straight down, other roots grow out laterally and branch out to hold the tree down, while very fine root hairs at the ends of roots take water and dissolved minerals and salts from the soil. If we could see this branching root system, it might resemble the structure and size of tree branches that we can see growing up from the trunk (as above, so below). Inside the roots, the tree changes the water into a liquid called root sap, which moves up the trunk in a layer of wood called the sapwood or *xylem,* comprising masses of miniscule tubes. Inside the xylem, root sap moves through the branches and out to nourish every leaf. Each green leaf is a little photosynthesis unit, which uses moisture and sunlight to remove carbon from the carbon dioxide in the air from which it makes sugars to feed the tree and oxygen to release into the air.

These sugars are then carried through strings of cells out from the leaves, outward and downward, to nourish the rest of the tree. These cells form a layer on the outside of the xylem, just beneath the bark of the tree, called the *phloem.* In between the xylem and the phloem, there is a thin layer of stem cell tissue, the *cambrium,* which runs from the leaves to the roots. All along the trunk there are medullary rays or conduits that link these elements with the outside of the tree, enabling the trunk of the tree to grow in diameter as the tree grows. The job of the cambrium is to create more xylem vessels on the inside and more phloem tissue on the outside. As xylem and phloem layers cease functioning and die, dead xylem becomes the heartwood, new xylem the sapwood, while the dead phloem is incorporated into the bark. Usually, new xylem is laid down in the spring and is wide and thin-walled; in the summer, the xylem is narrower, thick-walled, and dark in comparison with the spring xylem. These differences result in one growth ring per season. Having the cambrium close to the bark, the trunk of a tree can grow thicker year by year, some even for thousands of years.

My premed courses in college, medical school, internship, and residency were years of intense learning. There is an immense amount of information that a doctor of medicine needs to learn, and upon which we were tested, over and over again, with class rankings and the next rung up the professional ladder dependent on how much and how well we learned. Left out was the *wonder* of how the body was constructed and worked, or how the meeting of an ovum and sperm came with elaborate guidance on how to grow into a baby, or how a baby grows smoothly into an adult human being. There are glimpses of wonder along the way in the training of a doctor, but no one talked about such things. Wonder is all too often left behind in the process of becoming an adult, as well. When it is, an essential spiritual element is missing. We humans come into the world with a sense of wonder, expressed and seen most clearly in childhood.

Wonder is a precious sensibility to retain. Wonder and imaginative play go together in childhood and are together in the mind of creative adults who can be fascinated and enthralled by their new discoveries that then stimulate ideas and art. Wonder makes living on this planet an adventure. Then as we become aware of the vulnerability of life, some are called to save lives, others to preserve nature.

To grow like a tree is to be part of an interconnected mutually supportive circle of life: from soil to tree to water vapor to clouds to rain to soil and up again (the big picture) as well as a mini-ecosystem that sustains and nourishes this one tree. Whether as one tree on a hillside or one tree among millions in a boreal rain forest, this is so for every tree that lives naturally.

To spread the ashes of a loved one in the forest or woods, or under a special tree, or plant a tree in memory of that person is a ritual link to this large circle of life and also an actual link when ashes are spread or remains are buried: *ashes to ashes, dust to dust,* and dust to soil. The Earth prevails. What is left of our once-embodied selves, in turn and in time, will be incorporated into the planet. The fern forests and the trees gave us oxygen and nutrients to grow from a single cell into a human being, which we recapitulate in the uterus. Everything on Earth began with *her,* grew out of *her,* and will return to *her.* This is Mother Earth as womb and tomb, personified as the Great Mother of ancient and indigenous peoples: Our Mother who art the Earth.

2
GIVING LIKE A TREE

Inside our mother's uterus, each of us began as a fertilized ovum that grew into an embryo, then into a fetus, developing organs until they could be functional, gaining weight and size until, in approximately nine months of gestation, we were delivered into the world as a newborn baby. While inside our mother's body, we received oxygen and all the necessary nutrients to grow through the placenta that connected us to her physiology. In her body, she—our personal mother—produced the nourishment and eliminated the waste products of our metabolism, and maintained homeostasis, the steady environment in which her body's temperature, acid-base balance, and myriad other functions are kept within the range that sustains life. Mother Earth has been doing the same for us, and will continue to do so if we don't overwhelm her physiology with our numbers and toxic wastes.

As I learned about the evolution of trees and how Earth became a planet on which life was possible through the activity of trees, I realized that without trees, there would be no "Mother Earth." Earth, air, water, and fire—these basic elements—come through trees. Without trees, Earth would not have a breathable atmosphere, soil for vegetation to grow, or water fit to drink. Sparks would not become fire without oxygen and combustible matter, which trees continue to make. All life has grown out of the body of the Earth; evolution became possible because what is needed is provided. Earth in its abundance gives to us like a tree.

It is spring and I am in New Mexico editing and adding to *Like a Tree,* as I revise the first draft into its final state. There is a 120-year-old apple tree in full bloom outside the window; its white blossoms delicately tinted with pink are gorgeous. I think of how trees also provide us with beauty, and that this one in particular, a Wolf River apple, will provide a harvest crop of crunchy red apples, as well. Food right off the tree for people and horses that can be further transformed to last for many, many more months when they are canned. Spring-light green is the color filling out the once bare-limbed trees near the creek, trees whose roots hold down the earth, each part of a watershed, conserving water in its banks to be gradually released later, and preventing soil runoff from the sudden, infrequent thunderstorms. On hills above the creek and lining dry arroyos that testify to the existence of flash floods are the evergreen juniper and pine trees that cover the rust-colored hillsides in this high-desert country. So much of the beauty around us is created by trees. Here the tree landscape doesn't resemble that of Northern California, where I live. These are not like the redwoods in Muir Woods. It makes me realize how every tree in its own way is different and beautiful, as well as contributes to where it lives. This is, of course, a tree person talking.

The Giving Tree

I thought about the Wolf River apple tree outside the window, one among others that still remain from an orchard planted long ago, that has provided apples, beauty, shade, and pleasure and, in turn, been appreciated and tended. It is such a contrast to another apple tree, also on my mind: the one in Shel Silverstein's children's classic, *The Giving Tree*. There are lessons and choices for us in contrasting these two.

The Giving Tree is an illustrated book about a boy and a huge apple tree. It begins: "A long time ago, there was a tree, and she loved a little boy." He climbed the tree, ate her apples, took a nap in her shade. He loved the tree and the tree loved to play with him. As the boy grows older, he no longer comes to play. One day the boy returns to the tree and he looks sad. When the tree finds that the boy is sad because he wants money, the tree happily gives him all her apples to sell. Each time, the boy returns to the tree, he is older. The next time, he is a man and he wants a house. The tree tells him, "You can chop off my branches to build your house." The boy takes the branches and leaves happily. The next time the boy returns, he is getting old and wants a boat to go sailing and relax. The tree says, "Use my trunk to build your boat." So the boy does and leaves happily. Finally, after many more years go by, the boy, who is now an old man, comes back to the tree. The tree is sad because she is nothing more than a stump, and has nothing more to offer, but the boy says he doesn't need much anymore, just a place to rest. "Come boy, sit down and be happy," said the tree, and he did and the tree was happy. The end.

The story of the Giving Tree and the boy is troublesome. The relationship it models is natural and healthy only when a child is very young. An infant's needs and wants are pretty much the same, and when her baby is content, his mother *is* happy. A toddler who wants what he wants when he wants it, and is always indulged, becomes a selfish boy with a sense of entitlement, and if the pattern continues into adulthood, he will remain the narcissistic boy with the expectation that his mother and mother-surrogates will be his Giving Tree. Or, as we are seeing, *he*—as a symbol of human narcissism—will treat the planet as the Giving Tree, with the End being the end of the beauty and abundance of Earth as we know it.

Earth Photographed from Outer Space

In 1968, the Apollo 8 astronauts took photographs of Earth from outer space. For the very first time, it was possible to see the Earth as separate from us. We saw the beautiful sphere that is Earth: there were swirls of white clouds and the deep blue of oceans, and here and there, under the clouds, some brown and green that are partial glimpses of the continents. We saw Our Mother, the Earth, for the first time and she was beautiful. Seen against the vast void of space, she also appeared vulnerable.

Until we become adults psychologically, we see our personal mother (and judge her) in terms of how well she did or didn't meet our needs and wants. Only when we become mature can we see our mother as separate from our expectations of her, and at that point in our lives, she is aging and more fragile than before. If we are not narcissistic, we can see her as she is, love her, and realize that it is now up to us to take care of whatever she cannot do for herself. This is where humanity is in relationship to Mother Earth.

Trees and our Earth take such good care of us and all they ask in return is that we do the same for them. This beautiful home we all live on wants to give to us forever. But if we don't take good care of it and if we continue cutting down all the trees, eventually it will have nothing left to give us.

—JULIA BUTTERFLY HILL

Global Warming and Tree Forests

Mother Earth is a giving tree that has brought forth life of all kinds, including humanity, *Homo sapiens sapiens*, a relative latecomer. Once established and dominant, humanity has treated the Earth like the little boy in the children's book. Beginning with the Industrial Revolution, and especially since the mid-twentieth century, human beings have treated the planet, especially trees, like an inexhaustible resource. Individuals and corporations look at trees and see only their monetary value. With current machinery and technology, trees that took from years to millennia to grow can be cut down in very little time, carted to mills, and made into lumber, or brought to factories to become pulp and turned into paper products. A tree is then merely raw material.

Deforestation combined with population growth results in global warming, the effects of which are not immediately obvious. Human beings and institutions have heard the experts, seen the graphs and statistics, and respond in much the same way that individuals who are addicted to cigarettes hear but do not heed the necessity to stop smoking. The beginning effects of global warming are insidious and even disputable. The attitude is that there is nothing to get excited about even if the experts are right.

Once before, an alarm went off that wasn't initially heeded. This was the crisis over the proliferation of nuclear weapons in the 1960s. Some people then were like those that warn against global warming now, who think that people are reasonable and will respond to information. Numbers, statistics of those affected depending on how close or how far from ground zero, were given. There were photographs of mushroom clouds caused by nuclear bombs. Experts as well as activists in the beginnings of an anti–nuclear proliferation movement were speaking out. Children were taught to duck under their desks in school and people were building bomb shelters in their backyards.

In photographs of the Earth from space, our atmosphere can be seen as a very thin translucent blue layer covering the planet. These photographs move us by their beauty and the knowledge that this is our home planet. The photographs of Earth are in the shape of a *mandala*, the Sanskrit word for "circle" that has come to refer to Tibetan sacred paintings, and the geometric symbol as C. G. Jung described, for the archetype of the Self, the meaning-giving center of the psyche and a shorthand designation for the many names of divinity. All of which may have subliminally or subconsciously contributed to the effect of scientist and author Carl Sagan's words. He described how in even a very limited nuclear war, so much pollution would be sent into the atmosphere from the destruction that this lovely halo would become a dirty pall, preventing sunlight from reaching the Earth. The beautiful blue and white sphere that is our

Mother the Earth would cease to be an abundant, life-giving and life-sustaining planet.

If any country initiated a nuclear war and the other retaliated, radioactive dust and debris from the destruction would be sent into the atmosphere, and wind patterns would distribute this over the entire Earth. "Nuclear winter" would result. There can be no photosynthesis without sunlight, so all green vegetation and life that depends on vegetation for food would starve. Trees would die. Temperatures would drop. Earth would become a wasteland.

On top of the experts and activists that had sounded the warning, I think it likely that the beautiful photographs of the Earth as it is, contrasted to how it could be if the nuclear arms race continued, contributed to bringing that race to an end.

Now there are many other countries that have nuclear capability or are intent on acquiring it (Israel, Pakistan, India, North Korea, Iran). The situation is analogous to having stopped the growth of a potentially fatal cancer, which temporarily went into remission, and now finding that it has metastasized.

Global Warming and Tree Forests: Flying over Montana

When I traveled to the Feathered Pipe Ranch outside of Helena, Montana, I could see from the air the indirect damage to trees brought about by climate change. There were large swaths of reddish brown running through hills that used to be covered by green trees. Montana is called "Big Sky Country" for the visual impact of vast blue skies over mountainous horizons. Only now, it was more like flying into Los Angeles on a smog-alert day. Fires set off by lightning had hit parts of the forests that were now tinderboxes.

Once on the ground and driving up through Colorado Gulch to the ranch, I could see individual rust-colored dead lodge pole pines everywhere. The cause: the pine beetle that is threatening pine forests from New Mexico to British Columbia. It is the largest known insect infestation in the history of North America. Drought and global warming together have made trees vulnerable. The black hard-shelled beetle, the size of a fingertip, drills through pine bark and digs a gallery in the wood where it lays its eggs. When the larvae hatch under the bark, they eat the sweet, rich cambrium layer and inject a fungus to stop the tree from moving sap, which could drown the larvae. The tree's vascular system (the phloem and xylem channels) is blocked, cutting off nutrients and fluids. The Latin name for the pine beetle is *Dendroctunus ponderosae,* which means "pine tree killer."

To fend off an infestation, pine trees emit white resin, which looks like candle wax, into the beetle's drill hole. Sometimes the tree wins and entombs the beetle. Often, though, the attacker puts out a pheromone-based call for reinforcements and more of the beetles swarm the tree. In a drought, the tree has trouble producing enough resin, and is overwhelmed. As with infectious diseases in humans, whether a body is overwhelmed and succumbs depends on the strength of the body's immune system compared to the strength of "the bug," the virus, bacteria, or parasite.

Drought-weakened trees lose resistance and can't fight off an infestation as well as a healthy tree, and when winters are not cold enough to freeze the eggs, they will develop into the larvae that will kill the tree in the spring. The pine forests are dying as a result, and when they die, the fire hazard increases. Summer thunderstorms bring both welcome rain to green trees and lightning that can set off raging forest fires as dead pine trees are highly flammable. Flying home from Montana, just after the autumn equinox, I hoped for a cold winter, for snow and ice that would kill the beetle eggs that were probably already in the living pines I could see out the small window in the plane.

While my thoughts were on the green trees, I was seeing them through the air pollution. As trees burn, they send smoke and particles into the air, using up oxygen and releasing carbon dioxide, one of the major greenhouse gases, which traps heat in the atmosphere and contributes to global warming. The thinning and the depletion of the ozone layer caused by pollution from man-made chemicals (chlorofluorocarbons or CFCs) reduces the ability of the atmosphere to protect living things from harmful ultraviolet radiation, which causes skin cancer and cataracts in humans. Part of Patagonia at the tip of South America lies directly under the hole in the ozone layer, where hunters report blind rabbits, and fishermen catch blind salmon. Less widely known is that ultraviolet radiation affects the ability of trees to photosynthesize, diminishing the production of oxygen.

Easter Island

In *Collapse: How Societies Choose to Fail or Succeed,* Jared Diamond's description of what happened to Easter Island could be a scenario for planet Earth if we continue to cut down or lose the trees and the population increases.

(Diamond, a professor of geography at UCLA, was awarded the Pulitzer prize for *Guns, Germs, and Steel: The Fate of Human Societies.*) Easter Island is an all-by-itself island in the Pacific Ocean. Chile is 2,500 miles (4,020 kilometers) to the east; the Pitcairn Islands are 1,300 miles (2,090 kilometers) to the west. It is small, only 66 square miles (226 square kilometers), a mere dot in the vast ocean. It is now a barren place, famous for numerous mysterious and massive strange stone statues. These are look-alike huge heads with long ears and prominent noses and chins on legless male torsos carved from volcanic rock.

When Polynesian settlers arrived around 900 CE, Easter Island was covered with dense forests. There were twenty-two different kinds of trees, including the largest palm tree ever to exist in the world. We know about the species of trees from palynology, the study of pollen. Samples are obtained by boring out a column of sediment, the age of each layer is dated by radiocarbon methods, and then through tedious microscopic work, pollen is examined, counted, identified, and compared with pollen of known species. We know about the palm tree from fossil nuts that turned out to be very similar, but larger than those of the world's largest existing palm tree, the Chilean wine palm, which grows up to sixty-five feet (about twenty meters) tall and three feet (.9 m) in diameter. Fossilized casts of the Easter Island palm trunks and root bundles found buried in the lava flow from a few hundred thousand years ago proved that the Easter Island palm, with a trunk that was twice the girth of the Chilean palm, would have dwarfed it. While it existed, the biggest, most magnificent palm tree in the world could be found on Easter Island. Reading this brings to mind the threat to the old growth redwood trees in California, which are the tallest and largest trees in existence now.

The Polynesians who settled on Easter Island found trees that provided lumber to build houses, thatch for roofs, and strong rope. There were big trees whose trunks could be made into seagoing canoes, hardwood trees from which harpoons were made, trees that provided wild fruit and nuts, and the wine palm whose sap could be fermented. The islanders had all they needed to live well. They prospered, and as they grew in numbers, they used more wood and cut down their forests to clear land to grow crops as well.

Like Shel Silverstein's Giving Tree, the trees of Easter Island kept giving and giving until there was no more that could be taken. Once trees go, further loss follows. Through the hydrologic cycle, trees transpire water into the atmosphere and attract rain. Trees provide a habitat for birds, animals, insects, fungi, and microscopic life. Trees protect soil from erosion by wind and rain, and make more soil as their roots break rock into gravel and their leaves compost into organic matter.

The growth of the economy and the population growth based on what trees provided on Easter Island could not be sustained. Diamond describes how deforestation and wind led to a disastrous erosion of the topsoil. Six hundred years after the first settlers arrived, the population of Easter Island had grown to between six thousand and thirty thousand and there were more mouths to feed than food. Widespread starvation led to a descent into cannibalism and the population died off.

When the Dutch explorer Jacob Roggeveen came upon the almost deserted and barren island on Easter Sunday,

April 5, 1722, the few human survivors and the mute, mysterious, and monumental stone heads (the *moai*) were all that remained. The trees had *all* been cut down. Since Roggeveen first sighted Easter Island, there has been fascination, speculation, and fairly extensive study about the *moai*. There had apparently been competition between priests or chiefs to outdo each other in erecting larger and larger stone heads, as the size of the *moai* increased over time. There were hundreds in various stages of completion in the volcanic quarries, some were found as if abandoned near the roads, and every single one of those that had been erected had been toppled, many deliberately felled so that they would break at the neck. The *moai* were erected on elaborate, large platforms built of stone (*ahu*) and always faced inland. It's a surprise to learn that the heads that we see in photographs of Easter Island were re-erected much later, and never faced the sea as they do in the pictures.

Deforestation of Earth

Once upon a time, like Easter Island, most of Earth was covered with forests. Almost half of the United States, three-quarters of Canada, almost all of Europe, and much of the rest of the world were forested. Most of the deforestation occurred in Europe, North Africa, and the Middle East prior to this century. The United States was logged extensively. Most old growth forests, particularly in the East, were clearcut by 1920. Now old growth trees and forests are being cut at an accelerated rate in the tropical rain forests and boreal rain forests. Deforestation is a major contributor to global warming. Al Gore, in his 2009 book, *Our Choice: A Plan* to *Solve the Climate Crisis,* wrote that 20 percent of carbon emission is due to deforestation—more than the amount produced by *all* of the world's cars and trucks combined.

Easter Island is an extreme example of deforestation. People object to the idea that the islanders created their own downfall. Surely, they wouldn't be so foolish as to cut down all their trees, when the consequences would have been so obvious to them? Jared Diamond comments that this question nags everyone who has wondered how it happened, including himself. He writes: "I have often asked myself, 'What did the Easter Islander who cut down the last palm tree say while he was doing it?' Like modern loggers, did he shout 'Jobs, not trees!'? Or: 'Technology will solve our problems, never fear, we'll find a substitute for wood'? Or: 'We don't have proof that there aren't palms somewhere else on Easter, we need more research, your proposed ban on logging is premature and driven by fear-mongering'?" (*Collapse,* 2005, p. 114).

This imagined conversation echoes the rationalization to justify cutting down ancient trees by logging companies with profit as the sole motivation, and by the men hired to do the job. In developing countries, once the most valuable trees are efficiently harvested, the trees that are still standing are likely to be taken down for firewood or charcoal. On seeing the effects of deforestation when there is poverty, it is easy to see what happened on Easter Island: the trees became extinct, due to the deforestation that was done when the island was prosperous and then, later, when anything that could burn was used for fuel. Until one day, there was no tree left standing.

Like Easter Island, there is nowhere to go if we use up what sustains us on planet Earth. If we continue to pollute the water, use up resources, cut down the trees and the rain forests, destroy the ozone layer, turn fertile land into deserts, continue to create larger, more sprawling, more numerous and unmanageable cities—accelerating all of this through wars and the collateral damage that conflict causes to children and women, and trees, Jared Diamond's description of what happened to the people and trees that once inhabited Easter Island foretells what could happen to Earth.

Reforested Islands: Japan and Tikopia

Earth is a solitary island in space, analogous to Easter Island's position in the Pacific Ocean. Just as Easter Island can provide lessons in what not to do, two other island nations provide examples about how to avoid Easter Island's fate: Japan, an archipelago of islands; and Tikopia, one very small island nation. Japanese forests are now so well protected and managed that their extent is still increasing, even though timber is harvested from them. Despite the highest population density of any First World country, almost 80 percent of Japan consists of sparsely populated forested mountains. These are gorgeous green, primeval-appearing forests that cover Japan's mountains from one end of the island chain to the other, a forest mantle that inspires some Japanese to refer to their island nation as "the green archipelago." Though they appear to be primeval forests, most of Japan's accessible original forests were in fact all cut down by three hundred years ago, a time when the ingredients for a social and ecological catastrophe as happened on Easter Island or could happen on planet Earth were in place.

In *The Green Archipelago: Forestry in Preindustrial Japan,* author Conrad Totman describes the contrast between what could have been and what is: "Japan today should be an impoverished, slum-ridden, peasant society subsisting on a barren, eroded moonscape characterized by bald mountains and debris-strewn lowlands. Instead, it is a highly industrialized society living in a luxuriantly green realm" (1998, p. 1). Japan's affluence would be impossible without the ecological vitality of the island chain that has been sustained by centuries of effective silviculture. Silviculture, the branch of forestry to do with the development and care of forests, has the same derivation and sound as "sylvan," which refers to the woods or forest or to what lives there.

At the beginning of the seventeenth century, Japan was at a crossroad, with ecological disaster within sight. There had been construction booms and deforestation, soil erosion, decreased crops, periodic famines, and an increase in population, especially in urban centers. But instead of following the Easter Island scenario, over the course of the next two centuries Japan gradually achieved a stable population and reforested its land. Japan had the environmental advantages of soil and rainfall and a lack of sheep and goats to graze and destroy young growing green life, elements that supported nature's reforesting on previously logged land, plus the deliberate efforts by a succession of Tokugawa shoguns to preserve and grow trees and limit population growth during an era of peace. Under their leadership, the Japanese people were made aware of having a long-term stake in preserving their own forests.

A second island success story belongs to Tikopia, a *really* tiny (1.8 square miles or 4.66 square kilometers) and isolated tropical island in the South Pacific, which Jared Diamond cites as a bottom-up success story of forest management, population stability, and sustainability over three hundred years. Approached from the sea, this island appears to be covered by a multistoried rain forest, like those on uninhabited islands. Turns out that the nature-made rain forest is confined to a few patches on the steepest cliffs. The rest of the rain forest is a multistoried orchard, a forest in which every plant and tree is there because it produces edible food or is of use. This is an island with chiefs who serve as overlords over the four clans' lands and canoes, but from observation, the role of a clan chief appears to be as chief steward. At the beginning of the seventeenth century, the Tikopians made a momentous decision to kill every pig on the island. This is recorded in oral traditions and confirmed archeologically. According to these sources, their ancestors made this decision because the pigs raided and rooted up gardens, and competed with humans for food. I speculate that significance also lies in that this was done, even though pigs were a luxury food for the chiefs.

The tenacity with which men in power do not want to give up their symbols, perquisites, privileges, or the pattern of competitiveness among them, as they strive to build higher structures and bigger houses, drive more expensive and powerful vehicles or acquire nuclear weapons, or flaunt their wealth through conspicuous consumption makes this Tikopian decision highly unusual. Something is very different about the values of this culture and its male leaders. Tikopia is a *Giving Tree*, but the leaders of the island do not act like the *Little Boy*, which is so unlike most male leaders, whose "wants" use up all the resources. This has been especially so when the possibility of armed conflict arises between alpha males or warlords, who want more and bigger weapons, to display as well as use. There is *feminine* wisdom in the Tikopian psyche that took a long view and an overview in the matter of killing all the pigs. They had to have a caretaking attitude toward their resources and toward maintaining a population that could be sustained by resources, and vice versa. Women practice this sort of thing daily, juggling the budget or food available with the mouths to feed. When women have a say about becoming pregnant, they take resources and long-term needs into consideration.

The success of Japan's forest polices arose as a response to an environmental and population crisis brought on by the peace and prosperity of the 1600s. Beginning in 1570, the first two Tokugawa shoguns, Hideyoshi and Ieyasu, and their daimyo began to clear-cut Japan's forests for timber, according to Jared Diamond, "indulging their egos and seeking to impress each other by constructing huge castles and temples" (*Collapse*, p. 297). Shoguns then ruled Japan, the daimyo were their loyal barons, while the emperor became a symbolic figure. About two hundred castles were built, with towns growing up around them. The construction boom lasted from about 1570 to 1650, slowing down when timber became scarce. All old growth forests were gone by then, except on the steep slopes of inaccessible areas. Soil erosion had increased, the rivers were silted, watersheds disappeared along with the trees, the soil could not hold rainwater, which now ran off and caused floods. There was not enough food for the increased population and there were major famines after 1600. Japan's male power-elite had behaved like the selfish Little Boy in *The Giving Tree.*

All of this must have been similar to what happened on Easter Island. Initially, trees were abundant, clear-cutting for timber and space took place, and the population grew and increased the demand for more timber and resources of all kinds. Given the evidence of increasingly bigger and bigger statues *and* the psychology of competitive males, this would have required more human labor and the means to support them, and though the *moai* were made of volcanic rock, trees would be needed for firewood, rollers, scaffolds, and the ropes, without consideration of the cost to the people or environment. Probably there was competitiveness to please the gods or the priests and some theological rationalization for what they were doing. But in the end, the Easter islanders were left with a barren island and those strange male statues that they toppled. This brings to mind the replays on television of men toppling the statue of Saddam Hussein in Baghdad at the beginning of the American invasion of Iraq.

Medieval Japan was headed toward an Easter Island catastrophe. They got to the brink, and then, in the course of the next two centuries, pulled themselves back. In 1666, the shogun warned of the dangers of erosion, silting, and floods caused by deforestation. Tree cutting was reduced by a series of controls, the people were urged to plant tree seedlings, and by 1700 an elaborate system of forestry management was in place. Equally significant in avoiding an Easter Island scenario, Japan achieved a stable, zero-population growth rate in the eighteenth and nineteenth centuries.

Not Enough Trees, Too Many People

Not enough trees, too many people—this is simple arithmetic that, if unheeded, will take humanity over the edge into catastrophe. Earth currently has a population of more than 6.7 billion people, doubling since 1960, and is adding about 78 million people every year. There is a grassroots solution to the looming problem of overpopulation: educate women, provide information, contraceptives, and the freedom of choice. When women are educated and have reproductive choice, they delay their first pregnancies and have fewer and healthier children. It turns out that what is best for the individual woman and her children will collectively be best for the planet.

These are decisions that patriarchal men want to keep women from making. Efforts by the United Nations and NGOs to control worldwide population growth are unfunded or blocked by politicians, who follow what their religious leaders tell them. Consequently, there is active opposition to providing contraceptives even to avoid AIDS or after rapes, for family planning, and to efforts that give women the right to make decisions to do with their own bodies. The Pope and other Christian and Muslim male leaders who hold these same views have considerable political clout. The situation would be different if men got pregnant.

In the United States, political effort is directed at taking back reproductive rights that women gained in the *Roe v. Wade* decision by the U.S. Supreme Court. Since the 4th UN World Conference on Women, held in Beijing in 1995, the as-yet unachieved goal is for human rights and women's rights to be one and the same. Freedom of reproductive choice is an essential freedom for a woman because bearing a child forever changes her life and is a decision that determines whether a child is wanted and enters the world loved or resented.

A Woman's Right to Choose

Use of the birth control pill and the women's movement went hand in hand. "The Pill" gave women the choice whether to have a child and when, made it possible for a woman to have long-term educational or professional goals, or choose to be sexually active and not risk an unwanted pregnancy. The right to abort a pregnancy, which came with *Roe v. Wade*, allowed her to decide the course her life would take. She would not have to bear a child that began with a rape. She would not have to marry to make herself respectable and give an unwanted child legitimacy. She could consider the risk to her own health, or if married, the toll it might take on family resources. It is empowering and for most women also maturing, to have the right to choose and to live with consequences. Responsible women think in terms of the long-term consequences of every pregnancy, including the effect on other children or toll on the marriage.

"Another Pill That Could Cause a Revolution" was the title of Nicholas D. Kristof's column in *The New York Times* (August 1, 2010) and he speculated: "Could the decades-long global impasse over abortion worldwide be overcome—by little white pills costing less than $1 each?" The pill is misoprostol, a widely available drug that can't easily be banned because it is also used for ulcers and can save lives of women with postpartum hemorrhage. (In contrast, RU-486, mifepristone, is difficult to obtain in much of the world because it is used only for abortions.) When these two "M pills" are used together, mifepristone is taken first, misoprostol a day or two later. The combination results in a miscarriage more than 95 percent of the time in early pregnancy. Misoprostol taken alone is 80–85 percent effective, which is beginning to revolutionize abortion in developing countries where more than 80 percent of abortions take place, often under unsterile conditions that make the procedure dangerous. According to the World Health Organization, up to 70,000 women die a year from complications of these abortions. Kristof notes that this little white pill can be found on Internet sites and over-the-counter pharmacies in Delhi, where it costs just pennies per pill. The pill is taken at home, and produces a miscarriage that is indistinguishable from a natural one.

I don't doubt that news about this pill and how to obtain it will be widespread through women talking to each other. The means to prevent or end pregnancies outside the earshot of men has been a subject of concern to women—as long as women have known the connection between sex and pregnancy. Given the means, women will use them. At a time when the planet needs fewer people and more trees, the little white pill is good news.

In Japan and Tikopia, maintaining the forests *and* stabilizing the population went hand in hand. Whether it is a tiny island, a relatively larger one, an archipelago of many islands, or planet Earth, too many people for the resources is a recipe for social and ecological disaster. It is not enough to preserve and grow trees. Attention has to be paid to the birthrate as well, which women traditionally did when food was scarce or family size needed to be limited.

The leaders of Japan and Tikopia ceased doing what men who had been the shoguns or the clan chiefs before them had done. They resisted continuing to enact the *Little Boy* whose "I want" used up the *Giving Tree*. Lots of men—poor men as well as the rich and powerful—have this particular "Boy" in them. The lenders of microcredit loans learned this lesson. Initially, when microcredit loans began, the intention was to make half the loans to men and half to women. What lenders found was that most of the men spent the money on themselves or on impressing other men and didn't pay the loans back, while almost all of the women used the money to purchase what they needed to start a small business, made life better for their families and village, and paid their loans back. Now 90 percent of microcredit loans go to women. The "Boy" in men who need to impress other men built bigger and more castles in medieval Japan, bigger statues on Easter Island, and competed to build the tallest building in town, or in the world—with Dubai the current world record holder.

The Tokugawa shogun who began the reforestation was in the lineage established by the first Tokugawa shogun who ruthlessly took power after years of civil war, built Edo (Tokyo) as the new capital city, and with his daimyo used up the forests to build castles, shrines, and temples. I see parallels between these shoguns and the generation of ruthless American capitalists, the "robber barons" who established monopolies: John D. Rockefeller, J. P. Morgan, and lesser-known men who established great family wealth. It was their sons and grandsons, John D. Rockefeller Jr., Presidents Teddy and Franklin D. Roosevelt, and others with less noted names, who used their wealth and political connections to establish America's national parks, which have saved the spectacular wilderness and preserved the largest, oldest, and tallest ancient trees from loggers. In the absence of involved fathers, many of these men (of which FDR is most notable) were strongly influenced by their mothers and had summer homes in beautiful semi-wilderness areas, near water and forests.

It is now planet Earth and humanity that are at the brink of ecological disaster, and there are some optimistic indications that leaders and masses are getting the message. Awareness has been raised about fossil fuels, greenhouse gases, and global warming. Efforts are directed toward clean energy, recycling, and reducing our carbon footprint. All are logical means to reducing global warming, as are the efforts by conservation organizations to engage corporations to stop deforestation of the rain forests, or make deforestation a political priority. The 2009 UN Conference on Climate Change in Copenhagen brought leaders of the 192 member nations together to hear reports and speeches about the problem. The elite of the world are hearing the conservation message, international agreements and protocols to limit carbon emissions are emerging, but the political will to accomplish the goal is not likely until a critical mass of the public cares. Significant by its absence, the need to stabilize the population was not on the conference agenda.

Green Belt Movement

Saving the trees and forests, planting trees and new forests for the benefit of all, is not yet as high on the climate change agenda as it should be, but goals set in 2010 by the United Nations and non-governmental organizations may make it so. The realization that deforestation is responsible for more carbon in the atmosphere than all the cars and trucks that burn fossil fuels hasn't gotten much attention, even when Nobel Laureate Al Gore presents the facts and figures (see *An Inconvenient Truth* and *Earth in the Balance*). The Green Belt Movement in Kenya is a model of what can be done anywhere to restore deforested areas by planting seedlings on public lands, in yards, and on the edge of fields. The global Green Belt Movement has now set a goal of planting a billion trees a year; the Nature Conservancy and the UNEP also began campaigns to plant a billion trees. Bearing in mind that people who plant trees and take care of them develop feelings for them, I believe that involving children, boys and girls, will contribute to their becoming adults who love trees and Nature. The Earth Child Institute's new project—"2.2 Billion: The Power of One Child + One Tree = Sustainable Future for All"—is one example. It will connect schools or classes in one country with those in another. The children will learn about trees and people, and by planting trees, will be doing something that will actually help. Schoolchildren are doing something for the environment, together and tangibly, through Jane Goodall's Roots and Shoots organization, which began in Africa.

According to UN figures, 50 percent of the world's food is grown by women, a remarkable fact for us in the United States where farming is increasingly run by corporations, and referred to as agribusiness. In most of the rest of the world, where women grow food, planting trees would then mostly be done by women and girls, as in Kenya. But if planting trees becomes a project done in schools with computer links to schools in other countries, and if boys as well as girls would become involved in planting trees as part of maintaining the Earth's ability to take care of life on it, and if girls are educated to know the science behind what they are doing, the ripple effect could become a green wave. It is a simple concept: planting trees and tending them helps the planet. When we do so, we, as adults or children, become active participants in the cycle of life and the interdependence of life. The more conscious we are of what it is we do, the more meaningful it can become. To breathe in oxygen that the trees produce for us, and breathe out carbon dioxide, which they will take up and use, as a conscious act that connects us to the trees leads the mind to thoughts of interdependence, connection, and appreciation.

Andy Lipkis and the TreePeople

While I was learning about what is happening to forests and the people who save trees on far-away continents, I almost missed learning about the urban activists called TreePeople (one word) in Los Angeles, California. The organization was founded by Andy Lipkis when he was eighteen years old. At fifteen, he was at a summer camp in the San Bernardino Mountains where he learned from a naturalist that the trees in the forests around him were dying from air pollution creeping up from Los Angeles, and unless these trees could be replaced by a smog-tolerant species, within a few decades the trees would all be gone. It was 1970, the year of the first Earth Day. Andy did something about it. He and other campers planted a grove of smog-tolerant tree seedlings. Three years later, while in college, Andy was hard at work organizing hundreds of summer camp participants in planting thousands of trees. Thanks to a well-timed *Los Angeles*

Times article profiling his efforts to save 8,000 "baby trees" from being ploughed under by the California Department of Forestry, he received over $10,000 in donations, mostly in 50-cent increments. TreePeople was born, and Andy has served as its president ever since.

Since its founding, TreePeople's efforts have resulted in the planting of over two million trees in forests, urban neighborhoods, and school campuses. Over two million children have participated in its award-winning education programs. TreePeople has received numerous honors and awards, including recognition by the United Nations World Forestry Organization in 2003 for its work as a global model for other large cities. TreePeople has a citizen forestry training program, The Simple Act of Planting a Tree: Healing Your Neighborhood, Your City and Your World, which Andy co-wrote with his wife Kate. He is also working on using technology alongside healthy, well-cared for trees to create functioning community forests. "Technology" includes permeable paving, French drains, swales, rain barrels, cisterns, and other relatively simple "forest-mimicking" innovations.

Andy took on what I call "his assignment" when he learned that all the trees in his beloved summer camp forest could be gone in decades unless they could be replaced. He imagined this happening and was moved to do something about it. This is a path with heart that I believe that heart-motivated activists follow. I met Andy and heard him speak at this year's Bioneers Conference in Northern California and have no doubt that his story is an inspiring fit for my three criteria for an assignment: each new project from the very beginning was "meaningful, fun, and motivated by love." Lately, I have been thinking that to be an activist involves following intuition, persevering, and keeping faith that what you are doing matters, often in the absence of evidence that what you are accomplishing truly will make a difference when the cause is saving the planet.

The most exciting classroom I witnessed was outdoors. There were thirty or more young elementary school children on a field trip. They came from the city and were as diverse as a San Francisco public school can be. They were standing in a large circle, just outside the visitor center at the entrance to Muir Woods National Park. A park ranger-educator in uniform with his "Smokey the Bear" wide-brimmed hat was in the center of the circle. Every time the ranger asked a question, hands would shoot up. "Who knows who John Muir was?" "What is the tallest tree in the world?" "What else besides trees live in the forest?" These kids were having fun, were proud of what they knew already, and were taking in more information from the ranger. These kids were born after 2000, this will be their century, and the fate of the planet will be in their hands, soon enough.

The population of the world is very young now. Of the 6.7 billion people on the planet, 2.2 billion are under eighteen years old. Planting tree seedlings is "low tech" and takes patience. Every young person who does something for the environment, who loves the beauty of nature or even just one tree, or has felt a connection with the universe out under the stars may make a difference. A boy who cares for a seedling and sees it become a tree is in an alternative story to Shel Silverstein's *The Giving Tree* and is not as likely to become *that* Little Boy.

3
SURVIVING LIKE A TREE

"In many parts of the world, women are routinely beaten, raped or sold into prostitution. They are denied access to medical care, education and economic and political power. Changing that could change everything." These words, on the front cover of *The New York Times Magazine* (August 23, 2009), succinctly described the case made inside this issue, which had the theme: Saving the World's Women. The inspiration came from Nicholas Kristof, a *Times* Op-Ed columnist and coauthor, with his wife, Sheryl WuDunn, of *Half the Sky: Turning Oppression into Opportunity for Women Worldwide*. Their lead article was a summation of the case that the oppression of women worldwide is the human rights cause of our time, and their liberation could help solve many of the world's problems, from poverty to child mortality to terrorism.

Violence against women is universal. Amnesty International's 2005 publication *Stop Violence Against Women: It's in Our Hands* calls the statistics on violence against women a human rights catastrophe: at least one out of every three women worldwide has been beaten, coerced into sex, or will be otherwise abused in her lifetime. In any war zone, there is chronic stress, with heightened aggression, paranoia, and fear. Unemployment, killings, maiming, and loss numb people. It is then appalling but not unexpected to learn that over 87 percent of all women suffer from domestic abuse in Afghanistan, making it one of the most dangerous places in the world to be a woman. (UNIFEM, 2008–2009 Annual Report, p. 8)

Kristof and WuDunn wrote that a "bride burning" takes place approximately once every two hours in India, to punish a woman for an inadequate dowry or to eliminate her so a man can remarry, but this does not constitute news. Nor is it news that 100,000 girls in China were kidnapped and trafficked into brothels or that 130 million women around the world have been subjected to genital cutting (or FMG, for female genital mutilation). FMG is usually done when a female is young, varies as to how much mutilation occurs, inflicts pain, bleeding, and infection at the time, and later makes intercourse and delivery exceedingly difficult and painful.

Gendercide

The cover of the *Economist* (March 6–12, 2010) was black with the word "GENDERCIDE" in bright pink. Under this startling headline was the question "What happened to 100 million baby girls?" and "Killed, aborted or neglected, at least 100 million girls have disappeared—and the number is rising." When girl babies don't count, and prenatal sex-determination technology comes together with declining fertility, a skewed birth ratio of boys to girls is the result.

Normally, between 103 and 106 boys are born for every 100 girls. The ratio is so stable as to be a natural order of things, one that results in approximately the same number of young men and young women, because males are slightly more likely to die in infancy than girls. According to the Chinese Academy of Social Sciences, by 2020 there will be 30 to 40 million more young men than young women, because of the preference for boys. One in five young men will not be able to find a bride. Skewed birthrates for boys are found in parts of India, South Korea, Singapore, and Taiwan, and since the Soviet Union dissolved, there has been an upsurge in ratios of boys to girls in several former Soviet countries. In India in 2001, there were forty-six districts with a sex ratio of over 125 boys to 100 girls.

From the beginning, females vanish because they are selectively aborted, or don't get the same health care and food as boys. For example, in India, girls are less likely to be vaccinated than boys and are taken to the hospital when they are sicker. A result is that girls in India from one to five years of age are 50 percent more likely to die than boys their age. Women are the casualties of armed conflict; they are wounded, raped, or mutilated and subsequently die or are killed outright as collateral damage. Rape is a common gender hazard, but especially now in Africa, where rape of women is used as a weapon against men, to demoralize and humiliate them. Women die unnecessarily in childbirth without proper medical care.

Wherever there are large numbers of single men in countries where status and social acceptance depend on being married and having children, as they do in China, India, and most countries, a rise in frustrated single men leads to crime and violence in general, as well as abductions, trafficking of women, rape, and prostitution. This in turn leads governments to crack down on crime by being more authoritarian. In Muslim countries, older men with means who have have four wives as permitted by their religion add to the frustration. Unemployment and lack of education and opportunities for young men mean that they cannot afford to pay a dowry. These young men become a pool of recruits for terrorism.

Global Economic Crisis: The Effect on Women and Girls

By 2010, the context was a global economic and financial crisis on top of the ongoing crisis in food and energy. The World Bank estimated that as many as 53 million more people had been pushed into poverty as a result, and the International Labour Organization had warned that the number of unemployed women would have increased by 22 million. When families become poorer, girls and women suffer. An increased number of girls drop out of school, levels of violence against women and girls—domestic violence, human trafficking and sexual exploitation, with an increase in HIV/AIDS, criminal activities, and security risks—all affect what happens to girls. (UNIFEM/UNDP, "Making the MDGs Work Better for Women," 2009; Goetz, "Who Answers to Women?" UNIFEM, 2009)

Between what I have learned about diminishing rain forests and the plight of many of the world's women, it might be easy for me to conclude that this is not a good time to be either a woman or a tree, in a developing country or, for that matter, in many places in the world. Yet what comes to mind about women is a variation on the opening sentence of Charles Dickens's *A Tale of Two Cities*, "It is the best of times, it is the worst of times." For women who have benefited from the women's movement, there has never been a better time to be a woman. We have opportunities, freedom, education, and resources, and are living longer than any previous generation. We are living at a time when there is an emerging consciousness that both trees and women may be what can save the planet and bring humanity back from the brink. It is not just women in Western countries. There are women leaders in many developing countries who began working in NGOs. Through meetings often sponsored by the United Nations, they meet each other and are mentored and inspired and helped to have a larger vision of themselves. As a consequence, they step up to take on greater responsibilities.

Geometric Progression

The New York Times and the *Economist* were bringing mainstream attention to appalling statistics and personal stories of victimization, inspiration, and hope. There were facts and parallels to what I had learned or felt by being at the United Nations when the Commission on the Status of Women meets. I had become informed, my heart had been touched, and I had taken on a personal assignment of being an author-activist, a message carrier, through what I was learning. I wrote *Urgent Message from Mother: Gather the Women, Save the World* as a result. It is my belief that change comes through consciousness that grows collectively, one circle at a time and one person at a time. Through geometric progression, ideas can spread like a virus through a receptive population to bring about real change in attitudes and assumptions. It is what changed the world for women in the late 1960s, transforming consciousness-raising groups into the women's movement. It's "3 to the 19th power" mathematics: if three women learn something and each of them tells three others, there are nine. If each of these nine talks to three others, there will be twenty-seven. If these twenty-seven each pass on what they know to three more, it will reach eighty-one. If they, in turn, tell three others, in just four steps, the message will reach 243 people. In nineteen steps, it will reach more than a billion (3 to the 19th = 1,162,261,467).

When a critical number of people accept a new idea, the culture shifts. Whatever was resisted or ridiculed, or even condemned as against God's will—like the idea that women should have the right to vote—then becomes the new standard. The political struggle to gain women the right to a ballot in the United States took from 1848 to 1920 to achieve. The measure of success is when a right that was fought for is taken for granted: "Haven't we always had the right to vote?"

Trees Growing Out of Women's Heads: Betty Makoni

I first heard about Betty Makoni from Ann Smith, a Millionth Circle convener and cofounder of Circle Connections, while I was writing this chapter and was intrigued to learn from Ann that *Trees growing from the tops of women's heads* is a symbol for women and girls' empowerment. Betty Makoni is a thirty-eight-year-old African woman, a child abuse survivor, activist, and founder of the Girl Child Network (GCN) in Zimbabwe, and one of CNN's top ten heroes of 2009. Betty was raped when she was six years old by a shopkeeper who was known to do this to little girls. When she was eight, she tried to persuade her mother to report the domestic violence, and was told to be quiet. When she was nine, she witnessed her father beat her mother to death, and says she realized then the potentially deadly consequences of a woman's silence. When she was fourteen, her uncle raped her, made her pregnant, and also infected her with HIV (Risley, *Tapestries of Hope*).

The abuse Makoni suffered made her determined to save girls and women and become well educated in order to have a voice. She went to the university and became a teacher. When she noticed that girls dropped out of school at a very high rate, she gathered the girls who were still in school together, with the invitation, "Let's have our own space where we can talk and find solutions." This was the beginning of the Girl Child Network. By the end of that year, 1998, there were one hundred GCN clubs throughout Zimbabwe. By 2000, Betty had quit her job to devote full time to GCN and had started the first empowerment village as a haven for girls and women who had been raped. When girls are rescued and taken there, they are provided with emergency medication, counseled, and helped to return to school. Girls help each other in being transformed from victims to leaders.

Many men throughout Africa, including Zimbabwe, believe that a man with HIV/AIDS can be cured by raping a virgin, and Zimbabwe is the country with one of the highest incidence of HIV/AIDS in the world. This virgin myth cure is perpetuated by Zimbabwe's traditional healers. (The same supposed "cure" was responsible for European men infected with syphilis raping virgins, after the discovery of the New World brought this new disease to Europe.) As a result of this false belief and extraordinarily callous behavior, infected men in Zimbabwe have been raping girl children. According to UNICEF, hundreds of these little girls were too young to walk when they were raped. Betty Makoni said that the youngest rape victim was a day-old baby girl, who was too small to survive the penetration.

By the time, Betty Makoni was recognized as one of the 2009 CNN heroes, there were several empowerment villages and her organization had become the Girl Child Network Worldwide. Betty talks about how girls heal from trauma and of the symbol of a tree coming out of the woman's head growing roots that come from their resilience. The empowerment villages are an essential part of saving women and girls. Like the establishment of safe houses for women in America who needed to flee from abusive domestic violence, the empowerment villages become havens of safety and healing.

The Power of Women's Circles

When women and girls come together in safe conversational circles, truth-telling happens as they tell their own stories and hear others speak, and in the sharing, the recognition of commonality comes. Compassion for others is usually felt first, then compassion for oneself. Then there are discussions and ideas about whether to report the perpetrator and how to stop him from abusing other girls. This is where strategy talk begins: who will believe them and who might be trusted? Possibility of retaliation: what to do about this? How to mobilize the community and set up ways women can be helped. In these discussions, the psychological effects can be enormous. A shamed victim is transformed through this kind of experience into a leader. She has friends and allies, a home-base circle of support from which she can grow. Very similar to how consciousness-raising groups created programs and protests, and supported each other to become agents of change. By 2009, there were 30,000 girls in the Girl Child Network and 500 girls' clubs in Zimbabwe. The clubs create a safe place where girls meet with trained volunteers to break their silence. The clubs focus on five elements: identifying needs, mobilizing and developing strategies to go public on incidents of rape, leadership development of the girls, and developing and empowering the community.

Trees and Women as Hardy Survivors

Women and trees can be amazingly hardy, surviving under conditions that are unfavorable, sometimes extraordinarily difficult, as is true of the Peruvian huarango tree.

The huarango tree (*Prosopis limensis*) grows in the Atacama-Sechura Desert between the Andes and the Pacific Ocean. There a small grove of Peruvian huarango trees appears like a mirage amid sand dunes. In one of the driest places on Earth, the leaves of these trees capture moisture from the fog from the sea, while their roots are among the longest of any tree, extending more than 150 feet to tap into subterranean water. It is a hardwood rivaling teak. Its fruit can to used to make syrup, similar to molasses. The huarango is a giant relative of the mesquite trees in the American Southwest and it is on the edge of extinction. There are still some trees near Usaca that were alive when the Incas conquered the southern coast of Peru in the fifteenth century. That any ancient huarango trees have survived is a miracle, after centuries of systematic deforestation that began with the Nasca, who etched their mysterious lines in the desert a thousand years before the arrival of the Spanish. They cut down the huarango forests to plant crops, and exposed the landscape to the desert winds, erosion, and floods. There is a black market for huarango firewood and charcoal, which makes it a cash crop for woodcutters from poor villages and shanty towns who come at night with saws to harvest wood, ignoring the prohibition against cutting them down. Now a reforestation effort is under way, led by Oliver Whaley of London's Kew Gardens (John Walton, "Tree Planting in the Driest Place on Earth," *BBC News Magazine,* April 20, 2009).

Tree Huggers: Julia Butterfly Hill

There are people who try to save girls and women. There are other people who try to save trees, who are often called "tree huggers." Julia Butterfly Hill became the best known of them in Northern California—perhaps appropriately so, because women were the first "tree huggers."

In the late twentieth century, with the supply of redwood dwindling and the demand growing, the remaining groves of magnificent old growth redwoods in California on private property became very valuable. Pacific Lumber Company, a family-owned company that owned huge amounts of forest property, had acted like stewards of the forests, as they selectively harvested trees for decades. Then this company was bought by Maxxam, a Texas corporation, which set about clear-cutting these ancient, old growth redwood trees, bulldozing roads into these forests, and taking down groves of them. Tree wars waged between those who wanted to save the trees and those who intended to cut them down. These were conducted on the ground between loggers and activists, in the media, and through lobbying.

In the struggle to save the trees, in 1997 Julia Butterfly Hill joined environmental activists who were interfering with logging efforts by their presence and protests. She drew widespread media coverage after climbing 189 feet into the branches of a thousand-year-old redwood tree, and with activists on the ground providing supplies (they would be run off and come back), she remained in the tree she called "Luna" for 738 days. This was ad hoc activism. Julia, at age twenty-four, had traveled across the country to California, heard of the efforts to save the ancient trees, and showed up. When others climbed the trees so that they would not be cut down, Julia did also. While everyone else came down after short tree sit-ins, she remained for two years, becoming a symbol and spokesperson for the effort to save old growth redwoods. She tells the story in her book *The Legacy of Luna: The Story of a Tree, a Woman, and the Struggle to Save the Redwoods.*

When she was in her tree, the two of us spoke to an audience together—I in person, Julia via voice amplification with a phone connection from the tree. She was an engaging speaker; this plus her compelling story and the fact that she was speaking from high up in Luna in the middle of a forest made her a very effective advocate. She told us what it was like to be up in the tree on a 6′ × 8′ platform at night, of winter storms with high winds, and how Luna held her and taught her. *The Millionth Circle: How to Change Ourselves and The World* had just been published, and one example I shared was the Women's Sanctuary Forest circle, which was saving a grove of ancient redwoods through purchase and the commitment to raise the mortgage, while raising awareness by taking women to the forest and doing workshops there.

In 1999, the U.S. government paid to acquire the 7,500-acre Headwaters Forest of old growth redwoods, and negotiated an agreement for habitat conservation and a sustained yield plan on the remaining 211,000 acres on which there were twelve additional ancient redwood groves. This was accomplished through the efforts of Senator Dianne Feinstein during the Clinton administration and was a compromise that meant that some ancient trees would be spared but many, many more would become lumber (Julia's word was "annihilated").

Julia stayed in Luna for a time after the Headwaters agreement was signed, saying that it was "vital that I stay here because Luna and the Luna tree-sit represent all of the things left out or sacrificed, knowingly sacrificed, under this deal. By being here, I'm still able to tell people about the problems with the Headwaters deal." Julia came down from the tree only after the lumber company agreed never to cut Luna down and provided a small, permanent protected area around the tree. If she had come down right after the Headwaters agreement was signed or did not have a voice that the company wanted to silence, Luna would be lumber.

It was a forest and tree thing: Julia saw and cared about ancient redwood forests and loved one particular tree with which (or with whom) she had formed a bond.

Environmentalists who want to stop deforestation are called "tree huggers" by loggers. It is derogatory term, and is said with contempt that implies unmanliness and even a perverse sexuality toward trees: the implication being "real men don't hug trees." The phrase comes up when there are confrontations between men about saving trees. The epithet can be intimidating to men, a reminder of bad childhood schoolyard and street experiences of being called names, which went along with being bullied. "Tree hugger" doesn't carry an emotional charge nor is it directed toward women. Test it out: would you mind being called a tree hugger? Why does it or why doesn't it bother you?

When the homeowner's association called in the tree cutter to take down my Monterey pine, I did think of Julia Butterfly Hill. I also thought about picketing and getting media coverage, and with gallows humor said to some friends that maybe I should follow the example of women in India and chain myself to the tree. The association did schedule it to come down when they knew I would be away, so maybe the possibility that I might do something dramatic was not just my fantasy. It wasn't that I did nothing; I had gone to numerous meetings, hired a lawyer to help me know about my rights and choices, gone through county records, talked to a supervisor, made calls, wrote emails, and got the tree several reprieves. I was an activist on behalf of this tree, up to a point, which was reached. The tree would be down when I returned. I thought about the title of Alice Walker's book, *Anything We Love Can Be Saved*, and while this obviously isn't always so, I remain convinced that acting *as if it were true* is a good stance for me—on lots of matters. Up to a point.

Efforts to Save Oak Grove on the University of California Campus

Cutting down trees anywhere in the San Francisco Bay Area can be controversial. A long siege took place to save an oak grove on the campus of the University of California at Berkeley. It was a planned removal in preparation for the construction of a new student athletic facility. The grove was next to Memorial Stadium. According to an analyst from the California Native Plant Society, this was "one of the most outstanding examples of oak woodland in an urban interface, and the last remnant of coast live oak woodland ecology in the Berkeley lowlands." The grove consisted of about ninety trees: sixty-five oaks, eight redwoods, and others. There were three lawsuits, uncounted demonstrations, and a tree sit-in from December 2006 to September 2008, which ended when the grove was finally cut down. Feelings ran high, police were involved, and two chain-link fences were built. Oaks are protected by the city of Berkeley's ordinances, but the trees were on state property and exempt. Where I live, there are also tree preservation laws that don't apply to a homeowners' association.

While saving trees can be initiated by a protest, the protest itself often then becomes the issue. People in Berkeley as well as university students were reportedly evenly divided between those approving and those disapproving when polled about the demonstration. People care one way or another on most things, but just so much or not that much, and media interest moves on. Onlooker fatigue with both sides happens after a time, which is always to the advantage of the side with more resources. When an institution or corporation wants to cut trees down, it usually wins by wearing down the volunteer opposition. And, once the tree cutters prevail, this is the definitive last word.

The Chipko Movement: Tree Huggers

The first successful and publicized effort in which women saved trees from loggers was carried out by women in India, who did hug the trees they saved. It was called the Chipko movement; *chipko,* in Hindi, means "tree huggers." On March 26, 1974, a group of twenty-seven women peasants from Reni, a village in the Uttarakhand Himalayas in India stopped the local deforestation by hugging trees to prevent loggers from cutting them down. This was the landmark event of the modern Chipko movement. This successful nonviolent protest inspired hundreds of such grassroots actions and slowed down deforestation in India, and led to similar grassroots efforts elsewhere. Women in developing countries are the most directly affected and aware of the effects of deforestation because they are the ones who grow food, gather firewood, and carry water.

Within a decade, Chipko movement women had set up cooperatives to guard the local forests, worked on restoring degraded land, and established plant nurseries with species they select. The women also took on the social problem of alcohol and its effects. The contractors who paid loggers to cut down trees also sold alcohol to the men. Women who collaborate and work cooperatively talk about themselves and their lives, and what comes to the surface are problems that are generic to the community. The success that began as a desperate effort to save their trees had a far-reaching ripple effect. In 1980, the government issued a ban signed by the then prime minister, Indira Gandhi, against felling any trees in the Himalayan regions for fifteen years, until the green cover was restored.

Amrita Devi and Her Three Daughters

The historical precedent for Chipko occurred in 1730, when Amrita Devi and her three daughters were martyred. A local maharaja had sent his men to cut down the green khejri trees in her village. He wanted the trees to burn lime to construct his new palace. These trees were considered sacred by the Bishnoi, a Hindu sect to which she belonged. Amrita Devi resisted and reportedly said, "If a tree is saved, even at the cost of one's head, it's worth it." Provoked by her words, the loggers then used their axes to cut off her head. Her daughters were undaunted at what had been done to their mother, and offered their heads, too. In response to their resistance, the maharaja ordered the felling of all the green trees in the vicinity. News spread through the Bishnois, who were determined to save their sacred trees. Volunteers hugged the trees and sacrificed their lives. The loggers could not continue this slaughter, and reported back to the maharaja that they were unable to carry out their mission. By then, 363 Bishnois, young and old, men and women, married and unmarried, rich and poor had become martyrs to save the trees. The maharaja apologized for the mistake committed by his officials and prohibited the cutting of trees within the boundaries of the Bishnoi villages.

The khejri (*Prosopis cineraria*) was the sacred tree that Amrita Devi, her daughters, and the Bishnois martyred themselves to save. It is a small- to medium-sized evergreen, or nearly so, as it produces a new flush of leaves before summer. It has wonderful properties. Found mainly in the Rajasthan desert of India, it is frost-resistant and drought-resistant, able to withstand hot winds and extremes in temperatures. Its extensive root system stabilizes shifting sand dunes, it fixes nitrogen from the atmosphere into the soil and adds organic matter through leaf-litter, and it has a very deep tap root that can extend one hundred feet to reach moisture and so doesn't compete for water from nearby crops. Its leaves and pods are fodder for all livestock, and were eaten by people as famine food; reportedly, even the bitter-tasting bark provided sustenance. It provides shade and shelter, and can be a windbreak. Its wood is hard and makes excellent firewood and charcoal. It has a remarkable range of medicinal properties. Remedies are made from its flowers, bark, gum secreted in May and June, leaves, and pods. It truly is a giving tree, one that is now valued and protected.

Trees, Women's Circles, and Oxytocin

I saw a photograph of Chipko women holding hands encircling a tree to prevent it from being cut down and thought to myself that they had formed a women's circle with the tree at the center. Women in the Green Belt Movement in Kenya gathered in circles to learn how to plant and raise trees; the *idea* of a tree was in the center of their circles. In redwood forests, "daughter circles" of redwood trees can be found. These form years after a "mother tree" dies; in the past, this usually occurred after successive fires caused by lightning damaged the mother tree. New seedlings grew from tiny seeds released from the small cones by the heat of the fire around the perimeter of the ancient tree, or new trees grew from burls on the roots of the mother tree—for the root-crown can survive after the tree succumbs. There's a lovely daughter circle of redwood trees in Old Mill Park in Mill Valley, California, where children play. It has the feeling of a magic circle.

My book *The Millionth Circle* proposed that circles of supportive women who help each other, share an intention together, bolster each other's courage, and have a spiritual connection can change the women in the circles and change the world. The "millionth circle" is a metaphoric circle; it is the circle that when added to all the rest of the circles, creates the critical mass or the tipping point that brings the feminine principle and gender balance to the world. Though circles are a very natural form for women, the more circles there are, the easier it becomes for others to form, including mixed circles with men and circles of men.

There is an increasing awareness, which UCLA research on stress established, that when a circle or community of women face a difficult situation together, their natural response is to talk it over, which increases bonding and reduces the stress that isolated women would be feeling. This is called the "tend and befriend" oxytocin response, which is enhanced by estrogen (Taylor, et al., "Female Responses to Stress," *Psychological Review*, 2000). This is what women as a gender do, instead of the male "fight or flight" adrenaline-testosterone response.

Women as a gender have more neurological connections or fibers linking the right and left hemispheres of the brain, and can see different sides of a situation and different possibilities, including how everything could be connected, or perhaps and even more likely, how *everyone* will be affected. Much more often than not, women are geared toward solving the problem or getting the job done, rather than getting their way. When women speak up and can contribute to a discussion that takes into account the needs of all concerned, aggressive polarization is reduced.

Ongoing civil wars and conflicts, like gang wars in the neighborhood, are usually led by men who seek power and control, who are driven by fear of humiliation or fantasies of retaliation. The fate of the neighborhood or the world is then in the hands of psychologically adolescent, high adrenaline-testosterone men, who avoid any identification with weakness and aren't able to feel compassion. The oxytocin antidote to this is the power of women who come together to keep the children safe, who can draw upon "enough is enough" mother-bear energy, and work for peace when men do not see any way out of the conflict.

Such is the current situation in Gaza, the latest round in the nobody-can-win, Middle East conflict. If peace comes between the Palestinians and Israelis, it may come about when both sides are represented by women who are invested in creating substantive, sustainable peace and men who have the respect of their respective people and are wise. Patricia Smith Melton's *Sixty Years, Sixty Voices* profiles thirty Israeli and thirty Palestinian women who are open to talking with "the other." "Sixty" represented the historical anniversary that had created the divide. The Israelis celebrated the sixtieth anniversary of the State of Israel in 1948. The Palestinians lamented this date as the sixtieth anniversary of the *Naqbeh* (or *Nakba*), the catastrophe.

These women speak of the needs of the children and the need to stop violence in all forms. They believe that they do not need to love each other, but they believe that they can find a way to live peacefully and productively next to each other. They are examples of why women need to be involved in the resolution of conflicts: they have qualities and shared concerns, and are the gender best prepared to reach across differences, to build peace on mutual goals. This is supported by UN Security Council Resolution 1325 on Women, Peace, and Security (2000). Melton writes, "Since 1948, Palestinians and Israelis have suffered wars, *intifadas,* occupation, boundary changes, refugee camps, suicide bombers, failed attempts at peace, economic sanctions, prison detention, and sealed borders. Yet, the majority of Israelis and Palestinians say now is the time to come to an agreement each side can live with, an agreement that brings security, truth-based education, financial viability, and self-governance to both peoples." Melton asked repeatedly, "Is peace possible?" Every woman said yes. One psychological observation, for self-fulfilling prophecy: bring people to the table to work out peace agreements who believe peace is possible.

Every year, when Elana Rozenman comes to the Bay Area from Jerusalem, she invites women to do a Women's Peace Walk in Muir Woods through the serenity of the giant trees, walking slowly, silently with peace in every step. Women of different races, ages, nationalities, and religions have joined her, which I had done on two previous occasions.

In her email just prior to her 2010 trip, Elana described living "on the seam between Western Israeli Jerusalem and Eastern Palestinian Jerusalem" and told of a heart-warming incident between neighbors on different sides of the divide. After the death of Sarah, her son's mother-in-law, "the other grandmother of our wonderful twins," Elana set out for a walk through the Judean Hills to seek solace. "I met Fatima who is a neighbor from the Palestinian village down the street walking with her daughter," Elana wrote. "Even though she has little Hebrew and no English, and I have little Arabic, we always communicate deeply from our hearts and she has often seen me walking with my twin grandchildren. She greeted me with kisses on both cheeks, and immediately saw how upset I was and asked what was wrong. I told her that the twins' other grandmother had died and started to cry. She clasped me to her ample bosom and told me all we can do is accept what God/Allah is sending us and dried my tears with her hand. We each instinctively placed our hand on the other's heart and smiled at each other, kissed as we parted. I felt deeply comforted."

Northern Ireland

Catholic and Protestant women met together during "The Troubles" in Northern Ireland, the thirty-year period of violence, terrorist acts, construction of a wall, and British occupation. In 1976, Betty Williams and Mairead Corrigan received the Nobel Peace Prize in support of what they were doing. They were peace activists and cofounders of Women for Peace (which later became the Community of Peace People), who worked to find a peaceful resolution of The

Troubles. There were many other women involved in bringing peace to Northern Ireland, some of whom quietly contributed behind the scenes to the peace process negotiation, which brought about the Good Friday Agreement (April 10, 1998). Others contributed, as the Northern Ireland Women's Coalition party, to the success of the transition government. It was the three votes of this party that prevented the transition government from dissolving. I visited their offices in the imposing Stormont Parliament building in Belfast during the transition period; five years later, when I next visited, there was no trace of them in the directory. Working toward peace and creating a power base don't have to be mutually exclusive, but seem to be, especially with women.

Liberia

Ending the brutal years of civil war in Liberia—200,000 dead—was without hope of a sustainable peace until women became involved. Muslim warlords were terrorizing the countryside, while the Christian dictator ruled in the capital. Both sides warred on each other, with women and children the collateral damage. Muslim and Christian women did not make religion divisive; as they saw it, they prayed to the same god and, given their realistic fears and the suffering they endured, probably prayed for the same things. They joined forces, peacefully demonstrated, knew the young men who had been recruited and armed, and were a moral force who appealed to the international community, which responded. When efforts to achieve peace accords bogged down as the male leaders postured and enjoyed their accommodations, women barricaded the building in which the talks were being held and said they

would not allow the delegates out until they reached an agreement. The agreement was reached, after which the women
were, in effect, dismissed, and experts took over implementing it. The effort of the experts to disarm the belligerents
failed, however. Guns were not turned in, until the women
of Liberia who knew who had guns exerted their personal
moral force as mothers, neighbors, and relatives; this, along
with a financial incentive to surrender guns, was successful.
Christian and Muslim women continued to work together to
elect Ellen Johnson Sirleaf president. As of the beginning of
2010, she was the only female head of state in Africa (*Pray the
Devil Back to Hell*).

Sierra Leone

The secretaries-general of the United Nations, current and
past, have been men, often with well-developed masculine and
feminine qualities, which is true of all leaders with wisdom,
compassion, maturity, and moral authority. Documents have
been created at the United Nations that support and acknowledge the need for full participation of women in society. If,
for example, UN Security Council Resolution 1325 were followed, women would be involved in defusing the situation
leading to conflicts and would be a strong presence in every
peace negotiation. The advantage of having women participate is that women tend not to be locked into either-or thinking, use empathy to understand the other person's position,
and can compromise without losing face.

In Sierra Leone, the Sierra Leone Women's Movement for
Peace (SLWMP) helped to bring warlords to the peace table,
pressured by the United Nations, which used Resolution 1325 to

have women involved. Several peace talks and eruptions of the process continued between 1999 and January 2002, until the civil war was officially over. In March 2002, I attended NGO presentations at the meetings of the UN Commission on the Status of Women and heard women from Sierra Leone who had been directly involved in the peace process talk about it and about the years of meeting together (in what sounded like a large women's circle), at times staying connected with each other while some of them were in exile. One of the presenters described a warlord's outraged reaction on being pressured to have women involved in the peace process: his indignant comment was "What do we need the women for? You know that they would just make compromises!" The room of women broke out in laughter (Of course!).

Sisterhood and Trees: The Archetype of Artemis

Those of us who are involved in women's circles and women's organizations that have empowering or rescuing women and girls as their mission have a sense of sisterhood; otherwise it would not be meaningful to us to do the work we do. I hadn't thought much about these same women also being at home in the woods or having an affinity for trees, until I began writing *Like a Tree,* and at a meeting of the conveners of the Millionth Circle Initiative, spontaneously asked, "How many of you were Girl Scouts?" Every one of those present said she had been. Shouldn't be a surprise to me, though it was—confirming also that tree-hugging women and feminists are aspects of the same archetype, one that is personified in classical mythology as Artemis, the Greek goddess of the hunt and moon, who was most at home in the forests, glades, and mountains.

Artemis is the active archetype in feminists who have a sense of sisterhood, an egalitarian and competitive spirit, and a love of nature. Artemis was the Greek goddess who came to the aid of her mother when she was about to be raped and defended her honor when words demeaned her. She heard the prayers of a maiden to be delivered from her pursuer, saving her by transforming the girl into a spring. Women appealed to her for help in childbirth. Young animals were under her protection. In parts of ancient Greece, prepubescent girls were sanctified as "Artemis's Little Bears" for a year, protected from early marriage to older men. Whom she protected and the values she symbolized could define her as a feminist and an environmentalist. As goddess of the hunt, she could hit any target with her silver bow and arrows, and as goddess of the moon, she was comfortable seeing the world in moonlight and was identified with the crescent moon in its waxing phase, before it grows into its fullness. Artemis was a virgin goddess, while the Artemis part of a woman is psychologically virgin—like a virgin forest in her self-sufficiency and sense of intactness. Artemis was quick to act and decisive in responding to those who appealed to her for help, and also quick to punish those who offended her. Her companions were the nymphs of forest, lake, and mountains (Bolen, *Goddesses in Everywoman*, pp. 46-74).

Archetypal Differences

I was active in the American Psychiatric Association and headed the Council on National Affairs when I became an active feminist. The organization had held a referendum, which passed, to withdraw APA support of the Equal Rights Amendment. At the time, 89 percent of the psychiatrists were men, and two-thirds of our patients were women. Since inequality affects self-esteem and diminishes opportunities to develop, those of us within psychiatry who supported the ERA saw this as a mental health issue. With Alexandra Symonds, I became a cofounder of Psychiatrists for the Equal Rights Amendment and invited Gloria Steinem to come to the annual meeting in San Francisco: she responded, held a press conference, spoke, and got us media attention. We galvanized the convention with our bright-green ERA buttons, picket line, informational handouts, and Gloria Steinem. As a result, the Board of Trustees of the APA voted to support the ERA as many other national organizations were doing, by not holding its annual meetings in non-ratified states. In this case, the APA pulled the next meeting out of New Orleans (later rescinded) as well as made a significant financial contribution to get the ERA ratified.

I had thought that all women psychiatrists would support equal rights for women, but I was mistaken and learned from this wrong assumption: there are women who have a sense of sisterhood with other women and those who do not. I came to see these as differences in archetypal or innate patterns: between Artemis women and women who resemble Athena, the Greek goddess of wisdom, whose fine mind was put to strategic and practical use. Athena was the only Olympian that Zeus trusted with his symbols of power. In her mythology, she was born from Zeus's head, as a fully grown woman wearing golden armor. She's the archetypal father's daughter, who supported patriarchy and hierarchy. She was the patron of the city of Athens and of famous heroes.

In contrast, Artemis moved through forests and mountains, was not at home in the city or on the battlefield, where Athena was in her element. There are more than these two archetypes in women, but among those who are able to focus on a career and go through medical school, internship, and residency to get there, these two predominated and contributed to my understanding of the archetypes, which I based on the Greek Goddesses, when I wrote *Goddesses in Everywoman*.

Artemis women may have careers and causes, may receive recognition and gain positions in which they have power, but this usually wasn't the idea or the goal they had in mind when they struck a course into their particular field. Many NGOs are started by Artemis women, whose causes do follow those of the archetype, which would be to rescue or save those in need of protection (the environment, endangered species, animals, women, and children) or to empower them (women, girls, indigenous or marginalized people). The twelve areas of concern outlined in the Beijing Platform for Action and the NGOs that work toward implementing those goals are Artemis's causes.

Avatar: Tree People

While I was writing *Like a Tree*, I saw James Cameron's *Avatar*, which I viewed as a mythic confrontation between "tree people" and "not-tree people." It was science fiction allegory, took place on an alien green planet called Pandora, which was covered with trees and marvels of flora and fauna, much like a tropical rain forest with mountains, only more magical. These tree people lived in, below, and on trees; were indigenous folk, human in form, though much taller and with a graceful tail, and skin a lovely intense blue. They tapped into spiritual energy that came from Ai'wa, the Mother as a network of life. Like mystics here on Earth, the Na'vi experience a unity of consciousness or oneness with each other and all other beings, and all are manifestations of one Being, which they call Ai'wa. The greeting "I see you" is more than a surface hello; it is like the Sanskrit greeting *Namaste*, "The divinity in me beholds the divinity in you," which would be Ai'wa on Pandora. In reality, "I see you" is also an African Zulu greeting: *Ngiyakhubona* means "I see you."

The not-tree people were Americans, a corporate occupation of an alien planet, there to mine valuable ore. They had established a large base, with miners, mercenaries, and scientist-anthropologists. The anthropologists were learning about the indigenous people, the Na'vi, through their avatars. The crisis occurred when the richest amount of valuable ore was found to be under the immense and ancient sacred tree, the center or *axis mundi* (world center) of Pandora, a huge tree that held the community in it. The corporate manager wanted the avatars to persuade the indigenous people to move away from the tree and not cause trouble, before he ordered the tree to be destroyed, since killing them would be bad for the corporate image. But if they didn't cooperate, the necessity for profit made the decision clear. The tree was to come down.

The enormity of destruction of the towering, huge, and beautiful sacred tree filled the screen and was the beginning of the confrontation between them and the indigenous life of the planet. Destruction can be awesome and horrible. Such was the case. There is tremendous power and often skill involved in destroying something huge. Loggers who cut down ancient old growth redwoods and men who blow up buildings marked for demolition are skilled at what they do and take pleasure in it. I see a similarity to the pleasure that some little boys take in destroying the sandcastles others build on beaches, or the bullies in messing up the work of others they treat with contempt. In this film, the tall blue folks with tails have Mother on their side and, with the help of powerful animals, win this one. But as long as that really valuable ore is there, does anyone think that "the sky people" who "came from a planet where there is no green and killed their Mother" will not be back, this time with more troops and bigger weapons?

Superior firepower with no compunction about using it to destroy trees, animals, and indigenous peoples is the history of Western civilization—beginning with the invasion and conquest of the goddess-worshipping Neolithic people of Old Europe (25,000–5000 BCE) by the Bronze-Age Indo-Europeans whom archeologist Marija Gimbutas called the Kurgans, who with their horses, superior weapons, and sky gods, found the art-creating people of the goddess who did not build forts or elaborate tombs easy to defeat.

The contempt contemporary loggers have for "tree huggers" may go back to when divinity was the Great Goddess or, as Merlin Stone summed it up, "when god was a woman" and all nature was sacred. Indigenous people have held these same beliefs, as did the pagans of Ireland, England, and Wales. "Son of a Bitch!" referred to a man who honored and worshipped the Goddess (the Bitch); he was a pagan who honored Mother Nature. Men who are preservers of nature rather than destroyers deserve, in a positive sense, to be called, "SOBs," and may have been raised by mothers who instilled in them a positive attitude toward beauty and nature or helped them to develop the feminine aspect of their psyches.

The wealthy men who saved what are now America's national parks were motivated to preserve the beauty and grandeur of nature for everyone. These were the sons who inherited the wealth but not the same desire to amass more, which motivated their often-ruthless fathers. To preserve Yosemite and other wilderness areas, they stood up to men who were very much like their fathers, men who felt that it was their *right* to log, mine, and make money from nature. Preservation versus utilization (or exploitation) is what fights over trees are about. Greenpeace activists, the Earth First! demonstrators who supported Julia Butterfly Hill (one of whom was killed accidentally-on-purpose when a tree was felled to land on him), and the young men who occupied the oak grove at UC Berkeley have more in common with Artemis women than with dominator-males, which patriarchal cultures and families expect them to become. Boys and men who are allied with their own feminine nature and Mother Nature are like women and girls and trees, in that they are often put down and cut down psychologically. In those same parts of the world where male domination is the greatest and women are the property of men, suppressing the feminine in men goes hand in hand with oppressing women.

Bonds Between Trees and
Women Who Save Them

In the world where might makes right, where patriarchy is a warlord or corporation, very few people speak for the trees or tell of listening to them. Sometimes, however, one person's conversation with a tree can be lifesaving or mind-saving. One dramatic example, on which her survival depended, is told by Julia Butterfly Hill:

> Had I remained tensed for the sixteen hours that the storm raged, I would have snapped. Instead I grabbed onto Luna, hugging the branch that comes up through the platform, and prayed to her.
>
> "I don't know what's happening here. I don't want to go down, because I made a pact with you. But I can't be strong now. I'm frightened out of my mind, Luna, I'm losing it. I'm going crazy!"
>
> Maybe I was, maybe I wasn't, but in that moment I heard the voice of Luna speak to me.
>
> "Julia, think of the trees in the storm."

Julia pictured the trees bending and blown with the wind, as the voice of Luna continued speaking to her:

> "The trees in the storm don't try to stand up straight and tall and erect. . . . They understand the power of letting go . . . now is not the time for you to be strong, Julia, or you, too, will break. That is the way you are going to make it through this storm. And

that is the way to make it through the storms of life."
(Hill, *The Legacy of Luna*, 2000, pp. 113–114)

And so she did. Julia unlocked her tense muscles, she bent and flailed with the wind, howled and laughed, whooped and cried, screamed and raged. Once the storm was over, she realized that she had let go of all attachments, including to self and life and that people would no longer have any power over her: "I was going to live my life guided from the higher source, the Creation source."

Wangari Maathai's Green Belt Movement began with one particular tree in the heart of Africa. She told journalist Johann Hari that she would sit for hours under one particular fig tree, which her mother told her was sacred and life-giving and should never be damaged. "That tree inspired awe. It was protected. It was the place of God. But in the Sixties, after I had gone far away, I went back to where I grew up," she says, "and found God had been relocated to a little stone building called a church. The tree was no longer sacred. It had been cut down. I mourned for that tree. And I knew the trees had to live. They have to live so we can live" (Hari, "Can One Woman Save Africa?" *Independent,* September 28, 2009).

4
SACRED LIKE A TREE

At a State of the World Forum held in San Francisco a number of years ago, I walked into Grace Cathedral and heard
sounds from the Amazon rain forest playing through the
sound system—there were bird calls, animal sounds, and
other forest noises. Projected onto the pillars and walls on
the lofty church were photographs of the trees and life in
the rain forest. The light that comes through stained-glass
windows is dappled and, in this setting, it was as if coming through a forest canopy. For me, one sacred space had
been projected onto another—green cathedral upon stone
cathedral.

Often when I walk in Muir Woods, I have a similar feeling.
I am in a cathedral of trees, walking under the green canopy,
where here and there are patches of sunlight and sky. One part
of the forest is even called Cathedral Grove. Sometime during
my initial visits, the words of a summer camp song came to
mind: "I know a green cathedral, a hallowed forest shrine /
Where leaves in love join hands above, to arch their prayers in
mine / Within its cool depths sacred, the priestly cedars sigh /

and the fir and pine lift arms divine / into the clear blue sky"
(words by Gordon Johnstone, 1921).

When Joan Dunning followed the young people who
were her guides and for the first time entered into the old
growth forest they were fighting to save, her words echoed
these same feelings and more:

> Walking into Headwaters is like walking into
> Chartres. The forest is in charge of one's state of
> mind. The results of thousands of years of evolution
> envelop one's soul. The ability of the Earth to feed
> and clothe itself is glorified in greens and browns and
> reds—mosses, lichens, fungi, sing out the praises of
> decomposition while the varied thrush, the winter
> wren, the trillium, the yellow redwood violet, bring
> one back to the preciousness of the moment. What
> if Chartres had been bombed? Destroyed. I could
> never know completely what I had missed. Pictures,
> descriptions could not place one under the beams of
> that light penetrating through colored panes from
> forty feet above. It is the same with clearcuts and
> ancient trees (Dunning, *From the Redwood Forest,*
> 1998, pp. 64–65).

As noted, Anna Lewington and Edward Parker went on a
journey of discovery around the world to find and photograph trees that have lived over a thousand years, among
which are the redwoods. Their words are evocative:

> Imagine standing in a forest of giants, believing
> that every living thing has a spirit. Imagine looking
> up at the elegant spires of the coast redwood trees,
> with their uppermost branches wreathed in mist,

towering to over 300 feet (91 meters) above you. Imagine believing that the supreme creator under the First Redwood Tree made every living thing, and that redwoods are the guardians of the streams that provide the food on which you depend—the guardians of your very culture. For most of us it may be difficult to appreciate fully the reverence felt by indigenous peoples among these stately giants, but for the Tolawa people of the Pacific coast of California and Oregon such an awareness shaped their world for thousands of years before the arrival of Europeans (Lewington and Parker, *Ancient Trees*, 1999, p. 22).

The Tolawa and other indigenous people who lived among the redwoods were not able to protect the trees or themselves. Forests of ancient trees were cut down, whole areas were denuded, and many tribes became extinct when they were killed with impunity, once logging began. However, several thousand years before the Gold Rush brought fortune-seeking men to California, when Europeans lived in forests, they had similar feelings about the sacredness of trees. James Frazer, in *The New Golden Bough,* wrote, "From the earliest times the worship of trees has played an important part in the religious life of the European peoples. And, indeed, nothing could be more natural. For at the dawn of history Europe was covered with immense primeval forests, in which the scattered clearings must have appeared like islets in an ocean of green" (1959, p. 72). Within forests, there were sacred trees and sacred groves believed to be either inhabited or animated by spirits or deities. Often tribal communities lived in clearings, in the center of which was their sacred tree, which was also the center of their world. Trees were considered animate and therefore sensitive to being cut down. When the Roman legions attempted to subdue these tribes, one tactic was to demoralize them by cutting down their sacred trees.

Perceiving "Sacred"

In their introduction to *Ancient Trees,* Ann Lewington and Edward Parker wrote: "We have sensed the quiet power of some of the world's largest and oldest living organisms, and begun to understand the awe and reverence that many peoples in the past have felt. Standing in the presence of some of the world's oldest statesmen, it was impossible not to feel moved and reflect upon the transience of our own human lives; impossible not to feel that we are part of natural cycles that are just too large for us to comprehend" (p. 8).

Why are perceptions such as theirs so impossible for them *not* to feel, while others do not feel anything at all? Might this be a fundamental difference between a tree person and a not-tree person? Musing about such things, I thought about the difference between Julia Butterfly Hill and Charles Hurwitz, the Texan CEO of Maxxam who called in police to defend his property rights. He had bought the trees when he bought the land, and ownership gave him the right to do what he pleased, which was to cut them all down. It was the rule of law and Julia was a trespasser.

Tree protestors are not ignorant of the law, especially when the police are called in to enforce it. In defending ancient redwoods, they are like those in the rain forests or those who occupied trees at the University of California at

Berkeley. But preserving ancient groves is to save something of *sacred* value that once destroyed will be gone forever. "Sacred" is a perception that is not recognized by the rational mind, but by other ways of knowing. To *know* that "this is sacred ground" or that "this is a sacred object," or to feel "the presence of spirit," and to trust your own deeper sensing may be a fundamental difference between tree people and not-tree people. A tree is either an inanimate object of no value other than economic or practical, or it has a life force or presence of its own and is part of an animate world of which we are also a part.

Now that neuroanatomists have found neurons in heart tissue, Pascal's observation that "the heart has reasons that reason cannot know" may have a basis in anatomy: we may perceive and think with our heart as well as have ways of sensing subtle energies when the five senses of sight, hearing, taste, smell, and touch do not. "Sacred" perception in the language of theoretical biology would mean to be aware of the morphic field of the place, object, or ritual. In either case, receptivity on the part of the person is an essential element. By receptivity, I suggest that it is an attuning, a meditative attitude, a way of being in the present moment in which the chattering mind is silent. It's a simple principle, and it is what it takes to truly listen to music or to absorb what someone is saying with words while, at the same time, much more than words are sensed by a receptive heart or soul.

Anima Mundi

The world soul, *anima mundi* (Latin), or soul of the world is a concept based on a sensed or perceived experience of sacred unity. Plato described it as diffused throughout nature. It is what animates all life, just as the soul is thought to animate the human body. It is the underlying invisible oneness (Tao) that connects and underlies all the separate ten thousand things. It is a unity that connects all living things, all of which carry a spark of the *anima mundi*. It is the spirit or energy that makes a tree sacred. It is both an Eastern and Western concept that comes through mystics and contemplatives who perceive it. It is the Great Mystery, as indigenous North American people sometimes call it; or from the movie *Avatar*, it is Ai'wa. For others, it is the Divine Mother that is also the sacredness in matter. Once we perceive that there is sacred energy, spark, or spirit in everything around us, we realize that we inhabit a sacred world. For me, sensing sacredness evokes love and beauty and gratitude.

Aphrodite Consciousness

The mode of perception that opens the heart and mind of the perceiver through love is what I called Aphrodite consciousness and the alchemy of Aphrodite in *Goddesses in Everywoman*. When I wrote about the goddess archetypes, I was noting differences in their focus or lack of focus or the specific focus of each archetype; I put Aphrodite in a category of her own because of her "interactive field" of perception. It was neither focused (which examining something or aiming at something requires), nor was it diffuse and receptive (which allows a mother to hear the sound of a baby crying through a social din). Aphrodite was the Goddess of Love *and* Beauty in ancient Greece, and what we perceive through this archetype affects perception and response. Love is responsible for the saying "Beauty is in the eye of the beholder." When we love someone or something, who and what we love are imbued with beauty; there is a subtle energy in the field of attraction, communication, and response. This is the alchemy of relationship or communion with another. There is a similar principle in chemical equations: when two substances react, both are changed in the process. The "other" with which there is alchemy may be a person, a child, an animal, a bird—or for that matter, a tree or plants. This was how the Findhorn community in Scotland came to be.

Findhorn

The Findhorn Foundation community near Forres, Scotland, is the largest New Age intentional community in the world, with 450 residents and thousands of international visitors. It began in 1962, when Peter and Eileen Caddy, their three boys, and Dorothy Maclean settled in a trailer park near a rubbish dump on the edge of sand dunes and began to grow vegetables there. The land was dry and sandy, the summers in the north of Scotland very short, and yet they grew huge plants, herbs, and flowers—most famously, forty-pound cabbages. Other people came to join the Caddys and Dorothy.

Horticultural experts came and were dumbfounded. Word spread and Findhorn became a New Age community. The founders had followed spiritual guidance. Eileen Caddy had heard an inner voice that directed them to live there and start a garden. Peter's energy and intuition supported this. Dorothy discovered that she could communicate with plant spirits. Each species, it seemed, has an intelligence that knew what it needed from them to grow, and grow splendidly they did. Dorothy initially called them angels and then "devas" (*deva* is a Sanskrit word meaning "shining one"). Dorothy described them as "formless fields of intelligent energy" and said that they "hold the archetypal pattern of form" (Maclean, *Call of the Trees*, 2006, pp. 1–5). She did not hear words; she intuitively felt the connection, received the message, and then conveyed the meaning in her own words.

I described my initial visit to Findhorn in *Crossing to Avalon;* it was one of the places I went to on my midlife pilgrimage. Only after I took geography into account did I appreciate what others had called the miracle of Findhorn. The flowers and plants looked as if they were growing in sunny California, not in windy, chilly Scotland. By going there with the inner attitude and receptivity of a pilgrim, I also became invisibly linked (one attribute of a heart connection) to this community of people and nature that felt ongoing through unplanned meetings with Findhorn people. Many founders and holders of the Findhorn vision had dispersed by the time I visited, but our paths would cross. In the years to follow, I would meet Dorothy Maclean, David Spangler, Michael Lindfield, and Roger and Katherine Collis in California and Washington state. Katherine would become a Millionth Circle convener. Through heart-connected relationships, cross-fertilization happens. I keep finding that Jungian theory and analytical psychology provide an intellectual foundation that makes it possible for me to incorporate experiences and information that would seem far afield.

In this regard, I have thought about Rupert Sheldrake's morphic field theory in which every species has its own energy and intelligence field, and speculate that this field is what Dorothy Maclean may have "felt into." This may be what a deva or angelic presence or aura may be. In a message conveyed by, as she describes, "The angel overlighting the planetary work done at Findhorn," she learned "there are no individual egos with us. When you love one beech tree, for example, you love all beech trees, you are connected with the whole genus of beech" and "automatically linked up with the soul of that species" (*Call of the Trees*, p. 8).

At the beginning, she mostly learned and passed on practical knowledge of what each plant needed. Later, the messages from trees supported the living relationship between humans and nature and emphasized that large trees are essential for the well-being of the Earth. In one of many messages from the Tree Deva: "Mature trees are needed. . . . It is not enough to have the land reforested, for young trees are not capable of fulfilling our task of transmuting energy. You need us for this. . . . If there is a dearth of the large trees, the peace and stability of mankind is affected, for we are One . . . we have great inner strength to impart to you, and we will" (*Call of the Trees*, p. 76).

For all the people who have sensed such things, few among them speak of it until it feels safe or compelling to do. Many describe seeing spirits as children, and how adults couldn't see what they did. Perceptive, reflective adults who still remember insisted as children and know now that there was a difference between an imaginary friend and the real nature spirit they saw. If a child innocently speaks about what she sees and is told that it is "of the devil" or that she is crazy and is ridiculed, there will be no further mention or further development. An obedient or fearful child will turn away, as from a playmate who got her in trouble.

The Ethereal World

For some very sane adults, it comes as a distinct shock when an ethereal presence becomes visible or is a disembodied voice. People who are sensitive to such experiences can sometimes see ghosts or spirits. It's what I think of as non-ordinary reality, reasonable in much the same way that I can see that a dog is hearing something that I cannot hear myself. One can be measured objectively (sound beyond the hearing range of people but within that of dogs), and the other, while analogously similar, hasn't the science to back up the perception. In one such incident, an American tourist awoke to see quite clearly an ethereal figure of a crying woman in the room. She was surprised but not frightened, and spoke to the woman, who was in turn very surprised that she could be seen. They had a conversation, the details of which could be checked out in the light of day; the woman and her story fit into what was known to have happened a hundred years before.

Sharon Mehdi, author of *The Great Silent Grandmother Gathering,* was in Chartres Cathedral when she unexpectedly heard a woman's voice speak to her. Her first thought was "I must be crazy," and then, because of an inner certainty (*gnosis*) that she was hearing the Virgin Mary, she said to the voice, "You must be making a mistake, I'm a Methodist!" In spite of herself, Sharon was drawn back to Chartres many times to listen and learn, but it took her years to overcome her reluctance and resistance to share her experience, which she is doing now. Sharon is getting the messages she received out to others. She says that she can't convey in words what it is to hear the voice of the Lady of Chartres; there is something in the sound as well as the effect. I think that people, probably especially the very young, as well as animals and even plants can hear or receive something in a loving voice, and thus I can imagine that this quality would be amplified on hearing the Lady of Chartres.

I perceive the invisible world of energies through intuitive feelings, which the authors of *Ancient Trees* may have meant when they said that they could not help but feel reverence in the presence of very ancient trees. I believe I intuitively feel what more visually psychic people see as auras, or auditory ones may hear. I speculate that the saints painted stylistically on icons with gold around their heads were once actually seen that way. Their light was visible. With my perspective on non-ordinary realities, I have no reason not to believe the many accounts of people hearing celestial music, and maybe I will, too, someday. At sacred places, I sense where the energy is the strongest. This was a perception that I did not know I had until I went to Chartres Cathedral and felt something like a vibration or pressure in the center of my chest or heart chakra, which is how I sense, in my body, where energy is. According to Louis Charpentier in *The Mysteries of Chartres Cathedral,* Chartres has been a place of pilgrimage for several millennia. Prior to Christianity, it was the site of a Druidic sacred grove and a place of pilgrimage to a black Madonna carved from the trunk of a pear tree and a sacred well. The power of the site and my receptivity at the time brought this new ability into awareness and use. I think it likely that the more ancient the site or the tree, the stronger the invisible field. Many stone circles in England and Ireland, such as the one known as the Grange Stone Circle in southwest Ireland, have been in place for over three thousand years. These particular stones felt like wise and ancient presences that called me back to visit many times. None spoke directly to me, yet there was something compelling and real enough for me to value and return to visit. Again, there is the alchemy—sacred sites might very well be "awakened" by us, if we go as pilgrims, not tourists, to give and receive energy there.

There are places closer to home that have energy, but not of the same depth or quality as these ancient sites. It may be that sacred sites are vessels of alchemical energy, where there has been prayer and worship and love, a giving and receiving reciprocity at such places. After several thousand or more years, this energy is more easily sensed—if one is attentive. Paying attention to trees as tree beings, my sense is that there are old-soul trees near where I live; a couple are distinctive large oaks that stand alone on a hillside overlooking the ocean, close by a large outcropping of serpentine rocks, as well as the towering ancient redwoods. Younger trees of these same species with slender trunks feel like young, lightweight presences, as do many ornamental or flowering trees. I may be sensing the life force or the aura of the tree, or the spirit of the tree, that others have seen as tree spirits. Plants and trees respond to people who care about them. The gardener with a "green thumb" probably talks to the plants and may even listen subliminally to what they need. Maybe all we need to do on seeing a plant or tree that is not doing well is to ask. The answer may just come to us.

Findhorn is evidence for me that it is possible for some people to communicate with plants, and the "proof of the pudding is in the eating," so to speak. It gives me hope that, even though most of the rain forest elders with knowledge of the medicinal use of plants are now in their seventies, their knowledge might not die with them. The scientific approach is that the healing properties of plants came through trial and error, felicitous coincidence, or even watching animals, which then became intellectual knowledge. I wonder how it was first learned that a particular plant could be used for a particular cure if a particular part of it was picked at a particular season, especially when the instructions are complex. In that women are the more psychic gender and that back in the eons of hunter-gatherer human societies, women were the gatherers—and the healer-herbalists, as they still are in many places in the world—I think it likely that much information came to them from the plants themselves.

If communicating with plants is possible, then even if those with knowledge of the medicinal properties of plants in the Amazon die without passing on this information, that information could be accessed again: *if* plants in the Amazon rain forest and the talent to communicate with plants survive efforts to obliterate both.

A Findhorn Synchronicity

I unexpectedly learned something I thought significant when I almost bumped shopping carts with Avon Mattison at the local Whole Foods store, which is off her beaten path. Avon is a cofounder of Pathways to Peace, a UN NGO, and has been a peace-builder, educator, and consultant for over thirty years, prior to which she was a U.S. Foreign Service diplomat. She is also a Findhorn Fellow and told me of being present at a gathering at Findhorn before the death of Eileen Caddy (August 26, 1917–December 13, 2006). New facilitators came to meet Eileen and to hear her speak of the founding of Findhorn, which is to say, to learn something of their spiritual lineage directly from the founding member who had been given instructions from source to settle there, by a voice she heard in meditation while in Glastonbury, England. The voice announced itself with authority: "Be still and know that I am God." Eileen later said she thought she was having a nervous breakdown but came to "love the voice as an instrument from the God within us all." This inner voice guided the community through Eileen from its founding in 1962 until 1971, when it stopped, though she would hear it on other matters.

During this gathering of the new Findhorn generation of facilitators, everyone went to the original garden, which hardly anyone still visited; it was the small plot behind the caravan in the trailer park, where the Caddys and Dorothy Maclean began the first organic garden and where a tree that they planted as a seedling was now fully grown. The tree became the center of a ritual that included burying a crystal under it. The anecdotal or apocryphal story that Avon, who was there, recounted: As they did this ritual, a spontaneous hush fell over the entire Findhorn community some distance away; everyone became silent without knowing why. Findhorn came into being because Eileen did listen to the voice, and others who joined in creating Findhorn recognized an authenticity that came through her. Not from logic or because she was an expert, but because there was "something" that she and others recognized and heeded. Eileen Caddy was awarded the MBE (Member of the British Empire), a high honor and recognition, by Queen Elizabeth II, "For services to spiritual inquiry."

In telling me the story of the gathering and how an inexplicable hush fell over Findhorn, Avon was visibly moved. She told me this story after I told her what I was up to, which was the writing of this chapter. Her response made me realize that one of my hopes for *Like a Tree,* is that it will stir readers to remember similar experiences: that *you* will remember sacred moments and soul connections with nature, trees especially. Avon's Pathways to Peace is the NGO under whose auspices I and other Millionth Circle conveners and advocates of a 5th UN NGO World Conference on Women register as delegates to the United Nations Commission on the Status of Women meetings. Until this conversation, I did not know that she had a connection with Findhorn.

Under the circumstances, this unexpected meeting was a synchronicity for me. "Synchronicity" is the word coined by C. G. Jung for "meaningful coincidences," the occurrence of an outer event with something of importance in the psyche of the person. "Meaningful" is defined as such by the individual who feels or sees the connection between these events. It is a subjective interpretation. Synchronistic events are like dreams when attention is paid to them. Both give feedback to the observer in us. Dreams and synchronicities sometimes clearly support what we are doing (this was the case here), or present obstacles or warnings either in the form of unpleasant events or the appearance of people who carry a negative symbolic meaning in dreams or reality. Sometimes as if to underline its symbolic importance, a person will dream of someone with whom there has been no contact or even mention for years, and then shortly after, a "chance" meeting occurs.

This meeting with Avon brings up another observation. There was a response in me as she told about the ritual and the hush. I believe that people (tree people) can recognize or feel when something sacred is being shared in a conversation and that these are sacred conversations. Something rings true; the details may not be clear or even matter as much as the inner truth of the event: something awesome happened, and as the story is told, another person can feel it. As Avon told me her story, she commented in surprise, "I feel angel-bumps as I tell you." I'd never heard goose-bumps called angel-bumps before, but in the retelling, she was back in time and place and I could feel how awesome and real the experience was for her, then and now. It was a privilege for me to hear this.

This same phenomenon happens in my consultation office when something is shared that has this same subjective quality. I'm a psychiatrist and Jungian analyst by training and practice, and have listened to people's stories for forty years. The psychiatric training focuses on pathology and most psychiatrists, I suspect, have not listened long enough to people who hear voices or music in their heads to differentiate between auditory hallucinations associated with a psychotic state in a fearful, delusional person (who will likely be helped by antipsychotic medications) and people who are speaking of an epiphany and are afraid that hearing a voice means that they must be crazy (which many psychiatrists will wrongly confirm). It's very important for the person who is having the experience and the psychiatrist to have some discernment. Persecutory, guilt-inducing, hostile voices who are instilling ideas to do harm are definitely not to be listened to, and if an individual cannot get away from them—the voices inside or such people—help is sorely needed.

Open to Mystery

Tree people are open to mystery, that is to say, are themselves something of a "mystic," which comes from *mystes,* the name given to the initiate into the Eleusinian Mysteries in ancient Greece. This openness creates the conversational field in which sacred experiences, synchronicities, and awesome dreams can be shared. These can be life changing or course changing when attended to, but no matter how powerful, they can be forgotten by people who become caught up in ordinary life. However, when recalled, even decades later, these recollections may be like seeds discovered in ancient tombs that could still germinate and grow.

People are often cut off from their own numinous sources of meaning by others who have an influence over them. Parents, spouses, peer groups, psychiatrists, and priests who dismissed them, at best, or condemned them as sick or evil, at worst, made these significant experiences go underground. However, whatever was cut off or dismembered from consciousness and consigned to the unconscious still lives and can be re-membered. I am beginning to see this emerge in people in their third phase of life, when once again the opportunity to define what is important to them presents itself. People approaching retirement in their sixties may have many more active years ahead. This can be a time to remember sacred or ecstatic experiences that let us know that there is more to us than our bodies and more to the world than what we ordinarily perceive. The world of meaning is invisible.

I've thought how that which matters most is invisible: love. Without love, babies can die of anaclitic depression, young children fail to thrive, adults feel empty of meaning. Love nurtures soul, and soul perceives and responds to numinous moments in which there is a deep sense of being in a loving universe. To remember these experiences brings back a connection with soul. Soul, like love, is invisible—and yet we humans seem to have an innate sense that we have a soul. I think that once we acknowledge that each of us has a soul, it means that we are spiritual beings on a human path, rather than human beings who may or may not be on a spiritual path. What we do here on Earth must matter.

Present-Day Inquisition

During the Inquisition, the first to be burned at the stake were the wise women, midwife-healers, who used plants to ease the pain of childbirth and herbs to heal. When women went into labor or someone became ill, the villagers sought their help. Many herbal remedies have medicinal properties, as they knew then and pharmaceutical companies found much later. The Inquisition was established in 1252 by Pope Innocent IV, and continued with officially sanctioned torture for five and a half centuries, until it was abolished in 1816 by Pope Pius VII. It has been called "the women's holocaust," with the number of women condemned to the stake estimated from over 80,000 (Barstow, *Witchcraze*, 1995) to 9 million (Dworkin, *Women Hating*, 1973).

While Dorothy Maclean and the Findhorn community are safe from the Inquisition, Roman Catholic women's religious communities are not. The same office that conducted the Inquisition (the Congregation for the Doctrine of Faith) is conducting an investigation of North American nuns. The Vatican announced in 2009 that there would be an apostolic visitation to investigate the religious life and beliefs of communities affiliated with the Leadership Conference of Women Religious (LCWR), representing about 95 percent of the 68,000 nuns in North America (Fox, "Vatican Investigates U.S. Women Religious Leadership," *National Catholic Reporter,* April 14, 2009).

This investigation was preceded by the denunciation of Reiki, Therapeutic Touch, Healing Touch, and Centering Prayer, which are among practices used by many Catholic nursing sisters and retreat centers affiliated with the Leadership Conference. Therapeutic Touch and Healing Touch are subtle energy therapies used to promote healing and reduce pain and anxiety. In Therapeutic Touch, the hands of the practitioner are placed a few inches above the patient's body with the intention of having a positive effect on the aura or bioenergy field surrounding the body. Reiki is a similar practice that began in Japan, in which healing energy or *ki* goes through the palms of the Reiki therapist to the patient. The purpose of Centering Prayer is to clear the mind in order to focus on the indwelling presence of God (rather than on the rosary or focusing on a scripture reading) and has much in common with Buddhist mediation. That such practices could be "of Satan" is a scary medieval accusation.

Perhaps that this would happen is not surprising. Pope Benedict XVI was formerly Cardinal Joseph Ratzinger, the theologically conservative Prefect of the Congregation for the Doctrine of Faith, who disciplined Liberation Theology priests in South America, whose Christianity focused on social justice for the oppressed poor against landowners and officials who exploited them and the North American Creation Spirituality founder, Matthew Fox. Fox was ordained in 1967 as a Dominican priest, and has a master's degree and a doctorate in spirituality. He wrote about the Christian mystics and creation spirituality, and his theology focused on blessings and joy (see *Original Blessing*, 1983, revised 1996). The first investigation, instigated by Cardinal Ratzinger, was taken up by the Dominicans, who cleared him of heresy. Later, Ratzinger exercised the power of his office to require that Fox voluntarily agree to be silent for a year to consider his errors. I heard him when he spoke for the first time, after his year of silence. He was not repentant. In 1992, he was dismissed after refusing the summons to appear in Rome to defend his writings. Two years later, Matthew Fox became an Episcopalian priest.

Trickle-Down Grace or A World Filled with Grace

On several occasions, Matthew and I were at the same event, such as those sponsored by Common Boundary, which for years held conferences exploring the common boundary between psychology and spirituality. One talk he gave has stayed with me. It was about how the world used to be filled with grace, which was accessible to everyone. Then the Church became the sole dispenser of grace, which was scarce and came only through sacraments. Those at the top of the Church hierarchy had the most access to grace, and only priests (who could only be male) could dispense it. This is now a world in which grace is scarce and "trickles down" to the parishioner.

But to indigenous people who retain their old ways, to children who for a time may see nature spirits, or to Dorothy Maclean who sensed the beings of light who told her how to grow the magical garden of Findhorn, everything in nature is alive and full of grace. To the Saami (known by the name given them by outsiders as the Lapps or Laplanders): "Every being in this world is connected by Spirit. . . . We do not distinguish between this world and the spirit world any more than we do between our selves and the other beings in this reality, including the Earth and the rocks, trees and other plant life" (Madden, "Passevara," *Parabola,* Spring 1999).

Anyone who has had a numinous experience or felt the sacredness of something as real, or felt at peace and loved in meditation or felt pain go away and healing begin through touch has had a spiritual but not a religious experience. It may be that the leaders of patriarchal religions honestly think that this could not be so, and that the only explanation is that women (and the exceptional man) must be deluded or followers of Satan.

Numinous refers to a feeling of the mysterious that is awe-inspiring, holy, or sacred, evoked by an experience that is deeply spiritual or mystical. It comes from the Latin *numen,* which meant a spirit that was believed to inhabit an object or a place, an invisible supernatural being that can become visible or audible to human beings. It is the invisible "something" that imbues a tree or a sacred grove and draws us to them, provided, of course, that we have a receptive sense (which the most rational of our species do not).

We human beings have an innate capacity to sense the *numinous,* which, I believe, does distinguish us from all other species and leads us to worship. Whether ascribed to a "god gene" or to the archetype of meaning (which we experience as spirit, god, goddess, higher power, the universe, the Tao, or the Self), the perception of something numinous, of sensing something ineffable and beyond words, evokes awe. It is a *gnosis,* an intuitive knowing that there is an invisible reality. Once humanity lived in a world of matter *and* spirit, in which humans were part of nature. This remains true among many indigenous peoples, and was true for Europeans until authority declared that Nature was inanimate matter.

It may also be that that authority to speak for God claimed by prophets and patriarchs of the major monotheistic religions is essentially a continuation of the ongoing theological turf war with the goddess that goes back to the invasion of Canaan by the Israelites around 1200 BCE. The Old Testament tells how Moses led his people out of Egypt to the promised land, which already belonged to goddess-worshipping people whose way of life had made Canaan into the coveted land of milk and honey. After the land and people were conquered, the prophets railed against the abominations of Asherah, Anath, and Astoreth as false gods. There is no word for goddess in Hebrew; these were the names of goddesses and the abominations referred to were images of the goddesses, shrines to them, and sacred groves on mountains where people worshipped. Asherah was the Semitic name of the Great Goddess. She was called the "Mother of All Wisdom" or, simply, "Holiness." In the Old Testament, "Asherah" is translated as "grove," without explanation that the sacred grove represented the goddess's genital center, birthplace of all things (Davies, "The Canaanite-Hebrew Goddess," in Olson, *The Book of the Goddess,* 1985). I had researched this for a chapter in *Goddesses in Older Women,* and this made me think about the sense of desecration and violation that was felt by the goddess-worshipping people of Canaan as their sacred groves were cut down, and relate it to the feelings of activists whose protests can't stop the clear-cutting of old growth ancient redwoods. When trees are cut down, then as now, to those who truly care about trees, a tree is not *just* a thing, but a presence. Especially an ancient one.

There is a perception of an interconnected universe that is shared by the mystical mind and the particle physicist. That which we perceive as matter is made of atomic particles or waves, molecules or energy that shift one into the other. In Eastern philosophy, all phenomena—people, animals, plants, and objects from atomic particles to galaxies—are aspects of the One. At the atomic particle level, the worldview becomes very Eastern and mystical: time and space become a continuum, matter and energy interchange, observer and observed interact. In deep meditation, in complex mathematical equations, in particle physics experiments, and in synchronistic moments, we glimpse an underlying Oneness in which we participate. This was the spiritual point of my book *The Tao of Psychology: Synchronicity and the Self.* Events that cannot be explained logically by cause and effect nonetheless happen, and when they do, there can be tingles up the spine. It is uncanny and comforting to feel in the moment, as if part of a caring and even divine universe. This is what grace feels like—something invisible, divine, alive, and beyond what our mind can explain logically or prove to the almighty Rational.

Gaia Hypothesis

James Lovelock is the leading proponent that the Earth is a living organism—the Gaia Hypothesis, named after the goddess Gaia. In ancient Greek cosmology (Hesiod), she was the initial personified divinity who emerged from chaos and gave birth to the Sky god Uranus and everything on Earth as well as the gods and goddesses that preceded the Olympians. To consider Gaia as a living organism—or a living being—is to say that the Earth is "a self-regulating entity" that keeps our planet healthy by controlling the chemical and physical environment. The Earth, James Lovelock proposed, behaves as if it were a superorganism, made up of all the living things and their material environment. Gaia regulates such things as the level of oxygen, the formation of clouds, the saltiness of the oceans, and climate, which makes Earth a place fit for life.

Lovelock's thinking about Gaia grew out of his work on a project for NASA, on how to detect whether there was life on Mars. In thinking about Martian atmosphere (99 percent carbon dioxide), he contrasted it to Earth (0.03 percent carbon dioxide, 21 percent oxygen, 78 percent nitrogen), and realized that Earth's atmosphere had to come about through the activities of living organisms (bacteria, photosynthesis) and could be maintained only through their continuing activity. The study of how Earth does this, geophysiology, is similar to the study of homeostasis in human physiology, which has to do with how a healthy body maintains temperature and chemistry to stay within a very narrow range of fluctuation. Both are hugely complicated.

Detractors of the hypothesis that the Earth is alive rejected the idea: how could something be alive when there is only a very narrow band of life at the surface, that below this the Earth is composed of inert material, mostly iron? How could the planet be alive when almost all of it is inert or dead? Ancient redwoods are living rebuttals to this argument. Walk among them, there is no question that they are alive and, yet, the wood in the trunk of the tree is inert and not alive. There is only a thin rim of living cells protected by the bark that overlays them and, like Earth's atmosphere, protects the living tissues of the tree.

For Lovelock, humanity is part of the oneness that is Gaia; this is a holistic view in which everything on Earth is part of a living planet. It means that humanity shares the fate of the planet and contributes to it. Earth could conceivably have a natural life span that we are shortening, through the toxic wastes we create, deforestation, and the global warming that results. This is an environmental oneness that is not the same as the Tao, nor is it exactly mystical. While Lovelock's theory doesn't re-sacralize the Earth, it does reanimate it. "Mother Earth" comes back to life again when we perceive ourselves and all life as children of Gaia.

The Yew Tree and Allen Meredith

Ancient peoples believed the yew tree (*Taxus baccata*) was immortal. It was sacred to early Indo-European peoples, such as the Celtic and Nordic tribes, and symbolized ever-lasting life. Ancient yews have massive, complex trunks. "In the deepest winter months, it was not only green but often ablaze with flame-red berries and filled with the excited chatter of birds, an island of life in an otherwise barren land-scape" (Lewington and Parker, *Ancient Trees*, 1999, p. 68). As a species, this is an ancient tree. From specimens preserved in peat bogs, we know that yew trees were more numerous and widespread before the last Ice Age, which ended 1.7 million years ago.

The tree itself is exceptionally long-lived, with the possibility that a yew tree is the oldest living thing on Earth. It's possible that a yew tree might never die, because of the way it grows. It renews itself in several ways, which it does routinely, including from states of great decay. Its branches dip down to the ground, where they can take root and form a ring of new tree trunks around the original one at the center. After two thousand years or so, the tree's root system slowly pulls the trunk of the tree apart, exposing the heartwood, which rots and leaves a huge hollow that can be as much as ten feet (three meters) across. Once this center trunk splits, other branches can grow into the hollow, send down new roots, and form new tree trunks. From a scientific perspective, there appears to be no theoretical end to this tree, no reason for it to die. Dating age is a problem. It's impossible to find any one piece of wood as old as the whole tree, since most ancient ones become hollow. Growth is also uneven, as a yew tree can lie dormant for years. The yew doesn't grow to great heights, but is noted for its great age (five thousand to possibly nine thousand years old) and its great girth; one measures fifty-six feet (seventeen meters) The oldest known living specimen is the Fortingall yew in Perthshire, Scotland.

Much of what is known about the extraordinary longevity of the yew is due to Allen Meredith, whose study and preservation efforts became his lifework. He was not a botanist, but through his work, he convinced botanists that many yews are thousands of years old. His story and the information he uncovered are told in *The Sacred Yew* by Anand Chetan and Diana Brueton. Meredith had no interest in yew trees until he had a series of compelling dreams in the 1970s. He took his dreams to be a message that there was something he had to do. The dreams told him that ancient yews were dying from neglect and indifference (which his cataloging of all the ancient yews in Britain from his study of past records and from searching out all of them that could still be found in Britain revealed was true) because no one was aware of their great age (which his work and the support of respected botanists have now established). These dreams also warned that the survival of these ancient trees is linked to our own survival.

Meredith has been searching out yew trees, dating them through their history, uncovering data, and consulting with botanists since the mid 1970s. What he knows about yew trees and spent years validating came to him through dreams, intuition, and what he calls just "knowing." In 1974, he went to Broadwell in Gloucestershire to give a talk to some children about bird-watching. During the visit, the yew tree in the churchyard was pointed out to him, with the information that it was two hundred years old. He instantly "knew" that this was not right and that the tree was very much older. It was after this incident, which he would probably otherwise have forgotten, that he had the series of powerful dreams to which he listened and which set him on this course.

As I thought about Allen Meredith's story, I saw similarities to the founding of Findhorn. He received a message and knew (*gnosis*) that it was true: the tree was more ancient than conventional wisdom said it was. If plant-to-human communication and extrasensory perception (ESP) are real, someone who was (unknowingly) a "receiver" could *know* that what was being said about the tree was not true. It also established that there was a rapport between Meredith and the yew species. I think that when pilgrims go to ancient sites and get a strong feeling about what was once done there, or follow an intuition to honor the place by an improvised ritual, or have dreams that seem to come from this visit, many are receiving images and feelings from the collective unconscious (human morphic field) evoked by the place and the morphic field of the ancient place, stones, or trees. The yew is not only an ancient tree; there are reasons to believe that this particular species was the center of winter solstice rituals, that it still is symbolically—in a sense, remembered through Christmas trees. The yew may be the source of myths about sacred trees, including the various mythological Trees of Life.

Allen Meredith is also an example of someone who received an assignment or mission through his dreams and inner gnosis, who persevered, was helped by others, and is making his contribution. Subjectively, his " mission" is personally meaningful, turns out to be fun and creative, and is motivated by love for these trees, fulfilling my criteria for an "assignment." Love grows through commitment, and from this account of his life, his love for the yew, and his sense that what he is doing for the trees and for us, certainly has.

Other Sacred and Ancient Trees

The baobab tree (*Adansonia digitata*) is an African tree that grows to a stupendous size, its girth twice that of any tree in Europe, its shape bizarre in having a bulbous trunk, with bright green leaves shaped like a human hand. When these leaves fall in the autumn, twisted bare branches growing from a disproportionately wide trunk make them look like roots, which is why the baobab is often called the upside-down tree. It is impossible to know how old these giants are because all the ancient ones, like the yews, have hollow trunks. Among many native Africans, it is a sacred tree, believed to be the home of ancestral spirits. In one creation story, the first man and first woman were born out of this tree. A legend from the Bushmen is that the baobab trees fell fully grown from heaven, landing upside down. In the Upanishads, which are ancient Hindu scriptures, the cosmic world tree is Asvattha, an upside-down tree, which grows from the heavens and spreads its branches and leaves to cover the Earth.

The totara (*Podocarpus totara*) is the Sacred Tree of the Maoris. These trees grow on both the North and South Islands in New Zealand. The oldest known living specimen is the Pouakami tree on North Island, which is 1,800 years old, 12 feet (3.6 meters) wide, and 180 feet (55 meters) tall. The Maoris believe that these trees have a spirit and share a common ancestry with the Maori people, and that the ancient ones are elders. The kauri (*Agathis australis*) is another of the sacred trees of the Maori, another huge tree that grows on the North Island of New Zealand, the oldest of which is estimated to be 2,100 years old.

The olive (*Olea eropaea*) was sacred to ancient peoples of the Near East and to the Egyptians, Greeks, and Romans. In Greek mythology, it was a gift from the goddess Athena; for the Romans, from Minerva. The oldest known living specimens are over two thousand years old. The monkey puzzle tree (*Araucaria araucana*) is a rare Chilean tree that is sacred to the Pehuenche people of south-central Chile, who regard it as a "mother" and that it is their duty to protect this tree. The oldest living specimens are approximately two thousand years old. They have been declared a "national monument" of Chile and are an endangered species. The ginkgo (*Ginkgo biloba*) is revered by Buddhists in China and Korea and by followers of Shinto in Japan. They are temple trees;

the oldest known gingko is on the grounds of the Yon Mun temple in South Korea and is purportedly over 1,100 years old (Lewington and Parker, *Ancient Trees*, 1999).

Sacred as a Subjective Perception

It's special to walk in a grove of old growth redwoods, to pray or meditate in Chartres Cathedral, or to have the privilege of visiting sacred sites in the world, but only a very small percentage of people are able to do this—and then, many go as tourists. Even so, they may be touched by the invisible, ineffable "something" that seems to be there. I think that "sacred" is a subjective perception, something ordinary people come into the world geared to respond to or recognize and, if encouraged, is like any innate human ability or talent. It can be developed, remain latent, or be a human quality that is suppressed. Perception of the sacred outside of religion, and the mystical apperception of the interconnectedness of everything, however, has been particularly suppressed, across the board—discouraged in children and defined as craziness or superstition in adults or as heresy, which for hundreds of years of the Inquisition led to torture and being burned to death at the stake.

Most sacred trees have been cut down. Few ancient ones remain and they are endangered. However, "sacred trees" do populate the world of ordinary children. These are also endangered because children in cities and in the suburbs aren't meandering out of doors to find and return to their "secret place" or to their special tree as much anymore. I think back on Avon's story of the ritual at Findhorn, and it reminds me of how children bury their special objects or solemnly have services or rituals in their special places, or start secret gardens, and how bad they feel when a tree that mattered to them is cut down.

This is so for "tree people" of all ages, for whom trees matter.

5
SYMBOLIC LIKE A TREE

Standing between earth and sky, the tree is a symbolic link between the two. The role of priest, priestess, or shaman as an intercessory who stands between this world (earth) and the spiritual realm (heaven) is symbolically like a tree. Groves of trees have been sanctuaries of mother goddesses, fruit-bearing trees aspects of the triple goddess as the flowering maiden, fruit-bearing mother, and seed crone. Specific trees are spiritual symbols in Christianity (Christmas tree), Hinduism (the cosmic Asvattha tree), and Buddhism (the Bodhi tree). Druids lived in a world of sacred trees, where physical and symbolic merged. The tree can symbolize maternal qualities, as provider of nourishment and material needs, as in *The Giving Tree,* and protective shelter or home, as in a child's instinct to want a tree house. These are archetypal responses, connections made instinctively because they are drawn from a common source, the layer of symbols and patterns in the collective unconscious, which in turn draws from collective human experience.

Without trees, the planet would not have atmosphere, soil, and water. Trees have provided us food, materials,

shade, and shelter, and been havens of safety from predators on the ground. And when we stand and lift our arms to
the sky, as people naturally do in supplication or thanks, the
posture is that of a tree. The tree is a major symbol for the
cycle of death and rebirth in nature, with its yearly shedding
of leaves in autumn and renewal in spring. The evergreen
tree whose leaves remain green through the winter became
a symbol of immortality. The tree commonly symbolizes life
and growth, metaphorically representing a person's spiritual,
physical, or psychological development, which parallels the
biology of trees. Trees draw nutrients upward through their
roots from the earth and downward from the sun through
photosynthesis (incorporating light, symbol of spiritual
illumination). The image of a tree is a good visual metaphor
for people who are spiritually growing: be like a tree. Draw
insights up into consciousness from dreams with symbolic
roots in the collective unconscious; incorporate illumination from sacred teachings, prayer, and meditation.

To be like a tree is also about being in a collaborative
universe, not standing alone, but being in relationship with
all life, as the indigenous peoples consider themselves to
be. Alberto Villoldo, trained as a psychologist and medical anthropologist, studied shamanism in South America,
among people in the Amazonian rain forest who believe
that they can speak to the rivers and to the trees and to the
canyons and to the mountains and to God. Their shamans
believe that we live in a benign universe that will actually go
out of its way to collaborate with us, if we are in proper relationship with it, and that evil exists, but only in the human
heart. In their vision and understanding, each of us has a
luminous energy field that surrounds our physical body

(Church and Gendreau, *Healing Our Planet*, 2005, pp. 359, 363). In parapsychological research, Kirlian photography has been used as a means of producing images of this energy or aura. It is a photographic process in which people or objects are photographed in an electrical field with patterns of color and light visible around them. It's disputable what has been seen in Kirlian photographs.

Tree as Symbol of the Self

Trees that we remember from a dream or a myth, which then come into ordinary reality for us, take on meaning when we make the connection between the two events. That tree then takes on a special quality. An olive tree is just an olive tree, an oak just an oak, until a symbolic insight, a ritual, or a synchronicity gives it deeper meaning. A particular tree may be symbolically connected with a loved one or a mythic figure. Often a tree in Jung's psychology is a symbol of the Self, his name for the archetype of meaning, which is a generic term for the many ways in which we experience having a sense of purpose that grows from inside out. Connection with the Self is like having an inner compass that is drawn to divinity or wisdom as a lodestone, helping us to make choices true to who we are, to take one right step and then the next right step. Very often, the choice to be made is one of belief— between what we are told to believe by others and what we know to be true for ourselves.

In his essay "The Philosophical Tree," Jung summarized the usual meanings of the tree as a personal symbol: "The commonest associations to its meaning are growth, life, unfolding of form in a physical and spiritual sense, development, growth from below upwards and from above downwards, the maternal aspect (protection, shade, shelter, nourishing fruits, source of life, solidity, permanence, firm-rootedness, but also being 'rooted to the spot'), old age, personality, and finally death and rebirth" (*The Collected Works of C. G. Jung*, 1967, p. 272). He noted that in the East and West alike, the tree symbolizes a living process of enlightenment, and that if a mandala is thought of as a symbol of the Self seen in cross-section, then the tree would represent a profile view of it: the Self as a process of growth.

Jung's Personal Symbolic Tree

The tree as a symbol of hope, vitality, and transformation appeared in one of Jung's own dreams. During the midlife period in which he felt disoriented and sensed a loss of soul, he followed his dreams, visions, and active imagination, which took him into depths where he feared psychosis. He had had a series of powerful dreams in which an Arctic cold descended and froze the land to ice—all living green things were killed by frost in the first and second of these. In the third dream, the icy cold descended as before, but in this dream, he wrote, "There stood a leaf-bearing tree, but without fruit (my tree of life, I thought), whose leaves had been transformed by the effects of the frost into sweet grapes full of healing juices. I plucked the grapes and gave them to a large, waiting crowd" (Jung, "Confrontation with the Unconscious," *Memories, Dreams, Reflections*, 1963, p. 176).

As Jung comments, the tree in his dream is a symbol of his tree of life. This tree survived the icy cold. The ordeal had transformed it from a leafy tree into a fruit-bearing tree; its leaves had become grapes containing healing juices that he could pluck and give to the waiting crowd. This tree was an affirming symbol that came in the midst of uncertainty and anxiety. It held the promise that his suffering would have meaning, that it would bear fruit. We now know that his contributions to knowledge of the psyche, such as the collective unconscious, archetypes, anima, shadow, synchronicity, and much more, had their origins in this period of exploration of the psyche that he endured. The healing juices from the fruit of his tree of life are in his *Collected Works* and in Jungian analysis.

Tree as Personal Metaphor

Clare Peterson, who lives in Duncan, on Vancouver Island, provides an example of how symbol and person come together as a metaphor: "An image of a tree I drew once was a metaphor of my life. The roots tapped into and drank from the nourishing Spirit water deeply flowing below the surface of the earth. As I grew up, many different limbs branched from the trunk. Each limb represented a stage of my life. Some sprouted blossoms where I had made leaps in happy times and others were supported and bandaged from the difficulties and challenges along the way. Then at the top of the fir tree a small single seed pod burst forth and was carried into the major forest as my individual persona matured with purpose. I would become a part of the great forest of Earth, a successful completion and great joining. The ground was covered by all the leaves from all the life seasons of things, and the carpet collected on the ground became that which helped always to nourish me along. I loved feeling free as the little seed pod!" (printed by permission from personal correspondence).

Sometimes the metaphor of a woman as a tree is actually drawn as an image, which Penny McManigal did. Her drawing came from a very difficult time in her life "when the winds of life were blowing very actively, and I was trying to stay grounded. The realization that I am part of our dear Mother Earth helped resolve it." The drawing shows the outline of a woman, with roots holding her feet in place, while the wind tries to knock her off her feet (the wind is represented by a cloud with full cheeks and puckered lips). The wind is blowing so hard that her body tilts and her hair is streaming behind her. Yet hard as the wind blows, she is unmoved (printed by permission from personal correspondence).

The seed that led feminist-activist and author Deena Metzger to write *Tree* began with the shock of learning that she had cancer of the breast. *Tree* is in the same volume as *The Woman Who Slept with Men to Take the War Out of Them*. The image that comes to mind when I think of Deena is that famous poster of her found on walls of many women's clinics. She is triumphantly alive with her arms outstretched, face tilted upward bathed in light, one breast exposed and where the other had been, there is a beautiful tattoo of a leafy branch. I remembered her book as a cancer journal, and wondered why the experience was, in some significant way for her, like a tree. Deena wrote, "I named it TREE. The family tree. The Tree of Life." TREE is usually in caps in her journal entries and thoughts: TREE becomes healing light, healing love. She writes about sending and receiving TREE, how it can enter a person like a breath, be sent and received from afar, originates in the heart, and depends on the circle of people who are community. The branch winds about the surgical scar and travels from arm to heart. Green leaves cover the branch. She wrote: "On the book of my body, I have permanently inscribed a tree." This tree stands for TREE.

A Teaching from a Circle of Trees

Judy Grosch in Bernied, Germany, was on her daily walk when she chanced to look at a group of trees in the distance that she looked at every morning. On this particular morning, she saw them differently. "This is a grove of four majestic oak and beech trees. In winter they are handsome see-through individuals but today clothed in foliage they had become a new verdant entity lush with power that was radiating throughout the countryside. In that moment I received an understanding. When there is a group of living beings clustered together they are able to create something totally new that is incredibly more powerful than when they are separated. This new throbbing green being that these four trees had co-created told me that yes, it is important to come together for us humans thus creating a new entity pulsing with potential. And in addition, we humans have the great gift of intention. Imagine what we as a group are capable of doing! Imagine us connected together in groups around this planet bound in caring intention! Thank you, dear trees, for this important teaching!" (printed by permission from personal correspondence).

This is a very important teaching for spiritual activists who realize that their model for activism is not the lone hero, but the circle with a sacred center that is formed for a purpose. The "mother circle of the millionth circle," of which Judy is a member, does this. The Millionth Circle Initiative's intention is to seed and nurture circles with a spiritual center in order to cultivate equality, sustainable livelihoods, preservation of the earth, and peace; to bring the circle process into the United Nations non-governmental organizations and the 5th UN World Conference on Women; and to connect circles so they may know themselves as a part of a larger movement to shift consciousness in the world. Like Judy's seeing the trees together as something more and different from when they are separated, an ongoing circle has a history and a morphic field or energy that is more than the sum of the members who are attending. People can do more together than when standing alone. Activists, women in particular, know this.

World Tree as the Axis Mundi

The *axis mundi* ("world axle," the center around which the world revolves) is often symbolized as a tree, sometimes as a mountain or a pillar. It is a point of connection between sky and earth where the four compass directions meet. Here travel and communication between higher and lower realms take place; messages from lower realms may ascend to higher ones and blessings from higher realms may descend to lower ones and be disseminated to all. The designated *axis mundi*—world tree—was usually the most impressive and long-lived species in the geography of the area. It was an ancient oak to the Celts, the lime to the Germans, the sacred fig in India, the olive in Eastern Islam, and the ash tree in Scandinavian countries.

Yggdrasil: Norse World Tree

In Norse mythology, Yggdrasil is the world tree, an immense ash tree that links and shelters all the worlds, gods, humans, all living things, and is at the center of the world. Three goddesses, called the Norns, sit at the foot of Yggdrasil and weave the web of fate: Urd oversees past actions, Verdandi the present, and Skuld the future. They are similar to the Greek Fates except that they also keep the tree alive by watering it each day from the well of wisdom. Odin (Wotan) hung on the tree for nine days and nights in agony and sacrificed the sight of one eye, in exchange for wisdom—inner wisdom, insight, knowledge from runes.

The use of runes, Tarot, the *I Ching*, and other divination methods depends on synchronicity. There is no way to explain logically how these means could actually work. Runes use symbols from the ancient *Ogham* alphabet (Celtic Ireland), which is known from carvings on stones; they consist of one vertical central line (like a trunk) with "branches" that differ in number and direction. These were secret written symbols thought to be used by Druids, which may represent sacred trees as proposed by Robert Graves in *The White Goddess*, with each having its meanings and associations.

In Norse mythology, Odin is called all-father, and is known as Wotan in German mythology and in Richard Wagner's *Ring of the Nibelung*, the four-opera saga known as The Ring Cycle. Odin and Wotan are similar to Zeus in being the chief god, but differ from Zeus in ancient Greece and Jupiter, his Roman counterpart, in that Odin and Wotan sought wisdom and paid for it by the loss of an eye. Wisdom, as represented by the runes, is a means of knowing what is operating in the present from the past and is moving toward the future. It is intuition—associated with the feminine. I saw in Wagner's Ring Cycle and wrote in *Ring of Power* what happens when the acquisition and exercise of power become sought after and feared. The choice between power or love, when power wins, results in betrayal of relationships and a multigenerational dysfunctional family story. It is the underlying psychodynamics of patriarchy. The ash tree as an *axis mundi* is an important symbol that dies as a consequence of Wotan's actions. While it lived, the Earth goddess Erda dreamed everything into existence; what she dreamed would be woven by the Norns into being and anchored to the Ash tree. Then Wotan cut a limb off the ash tree and made it into the shaft of his spear, on which he engraved the agreements that he and others would be bound to; as a result, the spring at the base of the tree dried up and the tree itself died. Erda no longer dreamed. The feminine symbols as a source of life—the Norns, Erda the Earth Goddess, the ash tree, and the spring (sacred springs with healing and nurturing water were goddess sites in Old Europe, before patriarchy)—all became inaccessible.

Greek, Roman, Scandinavian, and German mythology all have sky gods who ruled from above, from Mount Olympus or Valhalla, as did the God of the Old Testament, who gave Moses the Ten Commandments on a mountaintop. The Judeo-Christian-Islamic creation story may be the only one, however, in which the masculine God birthed everything, including the feminine, and had no spouse. Sacred feminine and sacred masculine divinities were the rule until the Abrahamic religions and monotheism. In the others, divine wisdom is usually represented by a woman or by three women. Even in the Hebrew text, there is a feminine voice that can be construed as a hidden goddess presence (Sophia) in the book of Proverbs 8–9 in the Old Testament.

Asvattha: The Hindu Cosmic World Tree

The symbol of the tree rising through a number of worlds is also found in northern Eurasia and forms part of the shamanic lore shared by many peoples of this region. A central tree may be used as a ladder to ascend the heavens, and serve as a link between the visible world and the world of spirits. In the Upanishads, the sacred Hindu text, the cosmic world tree is Asvattha, an upside-down fig tree (*Ficus religiosa*), growing from the heavens and spreading its branches and leaves to cover the Earth. In the metaphor of the Asvattha tree, with its roots above and branches below, the Brahman (Divinity/God) is identified with the root. Each of its leaves is a song of the Vedas—divine knowledge—and it is said that he who knows one leaf knows them all (Jung, "The Philosophical Tree," in *The Collected Works of C. G. Jung*, p. 313).

Black Elk's Vision of the Cosmic Tree

Black Elk was a Native American Oglala holy man who spoke to John Neihardt in 1930. Neihardt was doing research into the Ghost Dance, and Black Elk and he became close friends. Black Elk gave him his life's narrative, including visions he had had, and some rituals he had performed. Neihardt's book *Black Elk Speaks* grew from their conversations continuing in the spring of 1931. In his Great Vision, Black Elk was shown many things by six Grandfathers—it was a panoramic and prophetic, long and detailed vision. At the time, Black Elk was nine years old. In one part of the vision, he was shown a great tree at the center of world, which is an image of an axis mundi or cosmic tree. Visionary artist and Arica

Institute teacher Jeanette Stobie painted Black Elk's vision as she envisioned it many years ago. The painting was my introduction to Black Elk, and made an impression on me, as art that is imbued with soul and is archetypal can do. Black Elk described what he saw:

> I was standing on the highest mountain of them all, and round about beneath me was the whole hoop of the world. And while I stood there I saw more than I can tell and I understood more than I saw; for I was seeing in a sacred manner the shapes of all things in the spirit, and the shape of all shapes as they must live together like one being. And I saw that the sacred hoop of my people was one of many hoops that made one circle, wide as daylight and as starlight, and in the center grew one mighty flowering tree to shelter all children of one mother and one father. And I saw that it was holy (Neihardt, *Black Elk Speaks*, 1961, p. 43).

Garden of Eden: Tree of the Knowledge of Good and Evil

The religions and mythologies of the world have significant trees in their "in the beginning" stories of creation and cosmology. Most familiar to us is the story of the Garden of Eden, in which were the Tree of Life and the Tree of Knowledge of Good and Evil. The familiar story: God tells Adam and Eve that they could eat anything in the garden except fruit from the Tree of Knowledge of Good and Evil. Eve listens to the snake, a conversation that leads her to eat the forbidden fruit and persuade Adam to do so also. As a consequence, they are banished from Eden, and prevented from ever going back: she is to bear children in pain and he is to earn his bread by the sweat of his brow.

Genesis has two parallel accounts of creation. In the first version (chapter 1), male and female were created together, both in the image of God, after everything else had been created. In the second account (chapter 2), the Lord God created Adam out of dust and breathed life into him, after which he planted every tree in the garden of Eden and when it was done, he placed Adam in it. In this version, Eve is created later after all the animals were made and named by Adam. God puts Adam into a deep sleep, takes a rib from his side and makes Eve out of this rib to be his helpmate. This text supports the patriarchal position of woman as man's subordinate, created from a part of his body, to meet his need. When Genesis was examined in the mid-twentieth century by scholars of style and language, they reached the conclusion that the reason for these two versions as well as other inconsistencies was that there were two sources (two documents were combined): one that referred to God as the Lord (*Yahweh*—singular), the other as God (*Elohim*—plural).

Elohim, the plural form, could include gods and goddesses and other divinities. The first chapter, first version of creation, begins with: "In the beginning, God (Elohim) created the heavens and the earth." Creation proceeds day by day, with a poetic cadence, repeating, "and God (Elohim) saw that it was good." After God (Elohim) rested on the seventh day, then Yahweh (Lord God, singular) appears in the text in Genesis 2:5.

The second version of creation in which Eve is made from Adam's rib is also where the Tree of Life and the Tree of Knowledge of Good and Evil are mentioned, along with the first prohibition: they are not to eat the fruit from the Tree of Knowledge of Good and Evil, "for on the day you eat of it, you shall die." The serpent told Eve that this was not so—she would not die, but her eyes would be opened and she would be like God (Yahweh), able to know good and evil. The tree itself is described as a delight to the eyes, the fruit was good food, and it was to be desired because eating it would make one wise. Eve ate the fruit and took some to Adam. When they ate the fruit, they knew they were naked, and sewed themselves aprons made out of fig leaves.

Before eating the fruit is a time of innocence and unconsciousness; in ordinary lives it's that happy time when children can run naked through the sprinklers, laughing and giggling in delight, before they learn about shame or predators and the need to cover themselves up. It is also similar to the beginning of puberty and the end of childhood, when girls and boys become aware of their changing bodies, may feel sexual yearnings related to these changes, and become self-conscious. Prohibitions and dire threats are part of parenthood and religion. Whenever emphasis is placed on that combination of temptation and threat, there is an inclination to test it. Then, there is the wait for lightning to strike, for the axe to fall, or for the Lord God Yahweh to carry out his threat.

Back to Genesis: Adam and Eve hear the sound of the Lord God (Yahweh) walking in the garden and they hide. The Lord God calls out to Adam, "Where are you?" and when Adam shows himself, the Lord God asks, "Have you eaten of the tree which I commanded you not to eat?" Whereupon

Adam admits to this but says it was the woman who gave it to him, and the woman says, "The snake beguiled me, and so I ate." Harsh punishment follows: Yahweh curses the snake, and places a curse upon the woman that became the justification for the punitive treatment of women by cultures based on monotheistic patriarchy.

Yahweh tells "the woman" (she is not given a name until after the banishment) that he will "multiply your pain in childbearing; in pain you shall bring forth the children, yet your desire shall be for your husband, and he shall rule over you" (Genesis 3:16).

And to Adam, Yahweh said: "Because you have listened to the voice of your wife, and have eaten of the tree of which I commanded you, 'You shall not eat of it,' cursed is the ground because of you; in toil you shall eat of it all the days of your life . . . in the sweat of your face you shall eat bread until you return to the ground, for out of it you were taken; you are dust."

When the Inquisition in Europe began, the theological justification to burn midwives was that they eased the pain of childbirth, which the Lord God had specifically decreed as punishment. Patriarchal marriage in which the wife desires only her husband (mandating virgin and faithful wives, allows the double standard) and the husband rules over the wife is based on these words. Laws in the United States in the mid-nineteenth century allowed a husband to use a stick to do this, as long as it was no thicker than his thumb. Repealing these laws, and the right to vote, were among the fifteen rights in the Declaration of Sentiments, 1848.

The Lord God (Yahweh) is the role model for the strong man in charge throughout most of Western history ever since. His behavior—to blame, lay curses, and punish when disobeyed—is a major theme in families, organizations, and history. The first point made by the Lord God Yahweh was that disobedience would be punished.

The second point, made in the story of Abraham and Isaac, is that obedience is rewarded. The Lord tests Abraham's obedience (some say his faith) by telling him to sacrifice his beloved son Isaac and offer him as a burnt offering on an altar that he and Isaac will make on Mount Moriah. As they are building the altar and gathering wood for it, the young boy in his innocence asks, "But, where is the lamb for the burnt offering?" (Genesis 22:7)—not realizing that his father intends to sacrifice him. Abraham bound Isaac on the altar and as he takes the knife to slay Isaac, an angel of the Lord calls to him from heaven not to do it, and provides a ram caught in a thicket for the sacrifice: "For now I know that you fear God, seeing you have not withheld your son, your only son, from me" (Genesis 22:12).

Eve's Choice

As a psychological choice, Eve chose consciousness. This is a choice that humanity keeps making, one individual person at a time. It is about the choice to think and feel for oneself, or not. It is the realization that good and evil exist in the world, because it exists in the human psyche. It is knowing and then taking moral responsibility for what we do, or don't do—for silence is then consent. It's learning to draw upon our own experience and apply intuitive wisdom. It is the opposite of what authoritarian regimes demand. It is the parent who says, "Do what you are told—because I said so, that's why!" Or the religious leader who says, "Because God says so and I speak the word of God."

Eve listened to the snake. The snake is a very powerful symbol connected to pre-patriarchal ancient goddess religions, such as on Crete with the famous image of a bare-breasted woman holding a snake in each upraised hand. Or Greece, where Apollo took over the shrine at Delphi after he killed the great snake at the sacred site of Ge (Gaia), the Earth goddess, and took control of her site of prophecy. The woman who went into a trance state and made predictions about the future kept the name "Pythoness," but her utterances were now written down (or edited) by Apollo's priests. The snake in the Garden of Eden can be thought of as a symbolic remnant of the demonized and suppressed Earth goddess. From ancient Greece to contemporary symbols of medicine and communication, the snake continues to be associated with divine messages and healing. Hermes, the messenger god of the Greeks, has two intertwining snakes on the caduceus he carried, while the staff of Asclepius the healer has one snake climbing it. At Epidaurus, snakes were kept under the floor of the *temenos*, the temple of the god of healing.

Myths about People Turned into Trees

There is another symbolism in Greek mythology in which people are turned into trees, so that a particular tree is a reminder of the story; the tree then symbolizes the person it once was.

Daphne and the Laurel Tree

The laurel (*Lauraceae Laurus nobilis*), known also as the sweet bay tree, grows wild in the Mediterranean region, and is related to the California laurel or bay tree, which thrives in parts of California. I see them growing in Muir Woods among the redwoods. It's an evergreen and is aromatic when crushed. Laurel leaves were used in Apollo's religious and prophetic rituals. Since the laurel is evergreen and produces no fruit, it is thought to be like a virgin, which Daphne was.

Daphne was the beautiful daughter of the river god and Earth, who wandered in the woods and worshipped Artemis, the Goddess of the Hunt and Moon. Or according to another tradition, she was a tree nymph and a priestess of ancient Delphi. Apollo, the God of the Sun, saw Daphne and fell in love with her. First he tried to woo her with fine words and his many accomplishments, but she was repelled by him and ran from him. This made Apollo desire her even more, and aflame with love and lust, he chased her through the country-side, across fields, into woods and marshes, "as a hound pursues a hare." Exhausted and about to be overtaken and raped by him, Daphne prayed to her father, Peneus, the river god, and just as Apollo grabbed her, her transformation began: a deep languor took hold of her legs, her soft breasts become enclosed in thin bark, her hair grew into leaves, her arms into branches, and her feet that had been so swift now were held to the ground by roots. She was transformed into a laurel tree. Apollo was devastated, wept, and made the tree his sacred emblem. In another slightly different version, just as Apollo was overtaking her, Daphne prayed to her mother the Earth Goddess, who opened the ground and received her, and in her place Earth created the laurel, which Apollo adopted as his sacred plant. One way or another, he possessed her.

From then on, laurel trees and leaves were used at all festivals in his honor, and crowns were made of laurel leaves to honor winners of contests. Roman emperors wore laurel crowns; Napoleon followed this custom and wore one of gold. Winning poets became Poet Laureates. The expression "Don't rest on your laurels" came from this myth and its association with Apollo.

Baucis and Philemon

Baucis and Philemon were an old devoted married couple who became trees. According to Greek myth, the gods Zeus and Hermes assumed human form and visited Earth disguised as poor travelers. When they reached Phrygia, they looked for shelter and were turned away by everyone except Philemon and his wife, Baucis. The old couple gladly shared their small amount of food and wine with the strangers. They realized that their guests were gods after noticing that the wine jug never ran out and that their poor wine was replaced by wine of the finest quality. After Zeus and Hermes revealed who they were, they led the couple to the mountain above Phrygia and sent a flood to destroy the land to punish the people who had refused them hospitality. A large lake now covered the land; only the old couple's cottage remained, which Zeus changed into a temple. He asked the couple what they wished. The old couple conferred and said that they wanted to live out their remaining years as guardians of the temple, and when the time came, they wanted to die together. One day as they were standing in front of the building, they started talking about the old days. Suddenly, each saw the other putting forth leaves. Their skin started to turn into tree bark. They embraced each other and cried, "Farewell!" Baucis was turned into a linden tree and Philemon into an oak, two different but beautiful trees intertwined with one another. In wonder, people came from afar to admire and hang wreaths on the branches in their honor.

Stories from Tree People

Betty Rothenberger read the introduction to *Like a Tree*, which I shared with conveners of the Millionth Circle, and was moved to respond: "I have always been a tree person, blessing the trees I see as I pass them in the car, cherishing the outline of individual trees against the sky, particularly at dusk when each stands out like a paper cutout."

Like Betty, I also see the trees I pass by, and take special notice of some in particular. I, too, notice the outline of the trunk and branches and shape of a tree. It has occurred to me that every time I see something beautiful, not just trees, my usually silent words—"How beautiful that is!"—are filled with gratitude that it is there and I am here to appreciate it. I think it's an instant thank-you—because I feel blessed by the experience. I wondered when I started noticing details about trees, and had a feeling that I am drawn to them, in part, because I began drawing trees when I was twelve or thirteen. Drawing a tree meant really looking at it. J. Ruth Gendler in *Notes on the Need for Beauty* observed, "Drawing becomes an act of regard, respect, reverence" (p. 23, 2007).

Betty also shared a personal story about Baucis and Philemon that is a wonderful example of how a myth can deepen experience by adding this dimension of meaning. In an email to me, she wrote:

> Some of my personal tree stories have to do with mythology and mythologizing my life. In front of

my house are two camphor trees (so they are ever-green, but shed their aromatic leaves in a continu-ing cycle), one on either side of my walkway to the door. I call them my Baucis and Philemon trees, because they remind me of the myth of the old and poor couple who welcomed and fed Jupiter (Zeus) and Mercury (Hermes) from their meager stores, and were rewarded by having their cottage changed into a shrine for which they were the custodians, and then were turned into companion trees at the entrance to the shrine when they died so that they would never be separated. These two trees shelter-ing the entrance to my home have made me feel I was living in and creating a temple here.

How much richer life becomes when the symbolic element enters into our experience.

In the following, Betty Rothenberger tells another tree story about symbol and synchronicity and the richness that being reminded of this brings (from personal correspon-dence and shared with permission).

Back in 1971 when I was dramatically called to Athena during a meditation [Betty has been a key faculty person in Jean Houston's Mystery School for years now], I determined to buy an olive tree in her honor. We were renting in Terra Linda then, so I put the small tree in a planter. Days after the tree was welcomed to the backyard, I came into the kitchen to find a live owl perched on the refrigerator. My husband was the one who was able to coax this wild one outdoors again, but I always took it as a message and affirmation from the archetype. Then when I divorced and bought this house, I planted the olive tree in the middle of the other half of the yard outside my bedroom window. It has flourished and by now is quite tall—and I look at it every day.

Trees as Individuals

Thomas Pakenham's *Meetings with Remarkable Trees* is an oversized book with sixty portraits and descriptions of trees. In his introduction, he remarks: "It is a personal selection of sixty remarkable individuals (or groups of trees), mostly very large, and mainly very ancient, and all with a strong personality" (1998). This is how he, as a tree person, describes a tree as a being, not a thing. J. R. R. Tolkien, author of *The Fellowship of the Ring*, took an appreciation of ancient trees one step further, into the realm of pure imagination, when he created the race of tree-like giants, the Ents, with Treebeard, the most ancient of them all. Ents came to resemble the particular trees that they guarded and had tree qualities. Older Ents often become "treeish," settling down in one place and growing roots and leaves. Eventually, they ceased to be conscious and became trees permanently. In either case, for men such as Pakenham and Tolkien, ancient trees have personalities and character.

Pakenham said he could trace the origins of his book to two experiences, "encounters, if you like": one at home in Ireland, the second on the borders of Tibet. He began the telling of his two "encounters," saying:

Now I don't usually hug trees, but on the evening of 5 January 1991, I made an exception. For three days the weatherman on Irish television had been tracking . . . a severe storm that would hit Ireland early in the morning of 6 January. I went out in the evening of the fifth and stood contemplating the old beeches in the garden. Nineteen of them. I guessed they were a little under 200 years old and 100 feet high. Why had I not looked at them more carefully before? The evening was absolutely still with the patch of red in the western sky that is supposed to delight shepherds. Pessimistically, I put my faith in the weatherman. I slipped a tape measure round the smooth, silver-green lichen-encrusted bellies of the trees and listed the measurements in a note-book. None was a record-breaker. But all had been good friends to five generations of our family. As I taped each tree, I gave it a hug, as if to say, "good luck tonight" (*Meetings with Remarkable Trees,* p. 6).

Gale-force gusts of wind struck the trees on the next day and night, "striking each tree or clump of trees, like a wave hitting the bow of a ship." When the storm was over, twelve of the beeches had been ripped out of the ground.

The second encounter Pakenham describes was with the first and last very large tree in the wild in the whole of Yunnan in southwest China, close to the border with Tibet in 1993. It was a Chinese hemlock (*Tsuga dumosa*) and so large that an old man had built a cabin among the roots. All of the other large, ancient trees had been taken down by the loggers. He was "meeting" the last survivor and a great presence, which made an impression.

Thomas Pakenham is a distinguished and award-winning historian. For this book, his research covered the length and breadth of Britain and Ireland. He found many ancient trees neglected. Besides introducing us to these venerable tree personages, he is an activist on their behalf. His advocacy and passion for these trees rings through the words he uses to address his native Brits:

> The indifference toward old trees makes a mockery of our supposed new respect for the environment. Consider the raw facts. The giants of our native species—oak, ash, and beech—are the biggest living things on these islands: heavier than any land animal, taller than most buildings, older than many ancient monuments. If a big tree was not a living organism it would still be a remarkable object. A big oak or beech can weigh 30 tons, cover 2,000 square yards, include ten miles of twigs and branches. Each year the tree pumps several tons of water out 100 feet into the air, produces a new crop of 100,000 leaves and covers half an acre of trunk and branches with a new pelt of bark. Yet the tree is alive. There is no mass production: every tree, sexually conceived, is built to a different design—as we see at first glance (*Meetings with Remarkable Trees*, pp. 18–19).

Considered fanciful initially, after the publication of *Meetings with Remarkable Trees*, Parkenham found that it struck a chord with the public; some wrote and said they had secretly hugged trees but had been embarrassed to admit to it. What Pakenham does, through his words, photographs, and love for trees, is convey what he feels for them to others.

He creates a "lens" through which others can see the trees through his eyes and, as a result, others may look more attentively to the trees around them. Or more likely, in speaking for the trees, he speaks for people who already feel an affinity for and personal relationship to particular trees. He helps "tree people" to own up that they are.

Tree Hugging

In going on the Internet to research "tree huggers," I came across Jenny Smedley's advice about tree hugging:

> If you would like to try a spot of tree-hugging, first stand still and find silence in your mind. Breathe deeply and concentrate on "feeling" the energies that surround you. Walk through the trees, and as you enter the aura of each one, ask if that tree is the right one for you. When you find the right one, reach out to it carefully, seeking the tree's agreement to the contact with you. Wrap your arms around the trunk and let your head rest against the bark. After a few seconds you may feel a soft vibration inside the tree. Reach into the tree with your spirit and bathe in its stream of life energy.
>
> Sometimes you will start to observe the world around you from the tree's perspective, and you may see the auras of the other trees around you, as sensed by your tree.
>
> Move away when you are finished, with consideration, for the tree will have been sensing your

energy too. Thank the tree, as you should always thank nature for giving you a beautiful experience, whether it be a rainbow, a sunset or just a wonderful view (Smedley, "Sacred World Series: Sacred Trees," *Merliannews*, 2005).

After reading about hugging a tree, did a *hmmmm*-thought, an "I wonder if?" about trying it come to mind? When nobody would be looking, of course. It takes courage to do something this foolish, though you could call it an experiment if someone catches you hugging a tree. What if you felt something—or though you didn't think you did, you then find yourself going back to the same tree to hug it again? Doesn't prove anything, except that you dare to be weird (from *Wyrrd*: in Norse mythology, fate personified by the three Wyrrd sisters or Norns who watered Yggdrasil, the world ash). If self-consciousness is a problem, sitting or standing with your back against the tree is both a respectable stance and another way to feel a connection to a tree.

Tree Meditation

In workshops, I often do a guided meditation, which varies, although there is one common element. Close to the beginning, I suggest, *"You will find yourself moving toward a special tree, one that may be familiar or it may be one that you are seeing for the first time."* Further along, I suggest, *"If your psyche is willing and you want to, you can merge with and, for a time, become the tree."* There are positive tree qualities that I want participants to feel as being about themselves: *"This is a tree that has been through many seasons and difficult times, may have had diseases, and could even have been hit by light-ning, and yet you survive and are unique and beautiful and strong. Its roots reach down, deep into the earth, its branches reach up high into the sky. It feels good, to feel the warm sun, to shelter others, to grow wiser."* I'm talking about being a tree and about them, blurring one with the other so that they can acknowledge these "tree" qualities as their own.

An invitation to do a guided meditation leads to a state of mind that is relaxed, receptive, and anticipatory, similar to how a listener becomes engrossed in a story that is being told. To begin with something as commonplace as a tree, and as deeply symbolic as a tree, is a good place to start. The guided meditation suggests, sets a story in motion for the person to fill in the details. Where might you be? Who might show up? What happens next? It is an invitation to tap into the imaginative, archetypal level of the psyche, where symbols come from when we dream. The symbols that show up when we dream are personal variations of the archetypes of the collective unconscious. These symbols, such as a tree, are found in many cultures and myths, over thousands of years. Then, as in our dreams, the symbol becomes person-alized; the tree that appears may be familiar, or special, and recognized, growing where? Representing what? By intro-ducing the tree in a guided meditation, people may realize or accept positive qualities in themselves that they ordinarily discount, and also tap into the deeper symbolic level to do with the meaning of it. When the tree is familiar, it is often a childhood one. It then can be a symbol of the child—who was close to nature—in the adult.

Many children who have a special tree have a *rela-tionship* with it. Sometimes when adults don't offer a child comfort, a tree can be there for the child: "Come sit by me and lean against me" is comforting. There is no need for the child to justify or explain feeling bad. A tree can just be there—for the tears and for whispered words. Perhaps it holds or surrounds the child in its energy field or aura. A psychological explanation is "projection"; the child projects the archetype of good mother or grandmother onto the tree. As with all projections, however, there is usually "something" that invites the projection. It may be the steady and peaceful aura of a large tree and the "hu" sound made by the breeze as it moves through the leafy branches that a child instinctively feels. There are good reasons for Nature to be called "Mother."

Richard Louv interviewed children for his book *Last Child in the Woods: Saving Our Children from Nature-Deficit Disorder*. A fifth-grade girl who wanted to be a poet told him how nature represented beauty and refuge:

> "It is so peaceful out there and the air smells so good. I mean, it's polluted, but not as much as the city air. For me, it's completely different there," she said. "It's like you're free when you go out there. It's your own time. Sometimes I go there when I'm mad—and then, just with the peacefulness, I'm better. I can come back home happy, and my mom doesn't even know why."

Then she described her special part of the woods.

> "I had a place. There was a big waterfall and a creek on one side of it. I'd dug a big hole there, and sometimes I'd take a tent back there, or a blanket, and

just lie down in the hole, and look up at the trees and sky. Sometimes I'd fall asleep back in there. I just felt free; it was like my place, and I could do what I wanted, with nobody to stop me. I used to go down there almost every day."

The young poet's face flushed. Her voice thickened.

"And then they just cut the woods down. It was like they cut down part of me" (2008, p. 13).

6
SOULFUL LIKE A TREE

I was reading the issue on gardening books in *Publishers Weekly* when an article title, "Branching Out," caught my eye. It asked, "Can publishers find room on their lists for an eclectic or whimsical title? If it's about trees, the answer for Susan Crittenden at Powell's Books is a fervent, yes, please. 'Vegetables feed the gut, but trees feed the soul.'" I thought to myself, of course! When I wondered why, a flow of thoughts, memories, feelings, and images came to mind. What started as a lighthearted question about trees and whimsical titles turned into "What is soulful?" to me. Answers came from tender, deep, wise places in myself. I realized that soul is drawn to what has soul.

Many trees are soulful. These are trees that are old enough and large enough to shelter us. These are the ones that draw out a stillness in us. Trees draw us to them—if we are tree people; they invite us to come inside (ourselves), into quiet. Once there is inner silence, there are sounds to be heard around the tree, which we usually don't notice. We may hear the wind blowing in the rustling of leaves, we notice patterns of light filtering through the tree canopy, we enter nature in the here and now, which is also the only way to be receptive to the soul within us.

Soulfulness and stillness are connected. In the midst of an ever-moving, overactive, busy world, the words from T. S. Eliot's *Four Quartets* describe when I drop into the soul realm. It is "in the stillness between two waves of the Sea" or "at the still point of the turning world." It is when we find that inner still point, which requires that we cease our activity and find quiet between waves of emotion. It is in the stillness that soul makes itself known. The soul speaks through a poetic phrase, or is echoed in a poem or through musical notes, that touches soul or expresses soul. Feelings and intimations are deepened by images and metaphors; soul acts upon us like a thread that tugs on us to remember, and be led back to where we touched into the eternal or archetypal.

Anne D. LeClaire's *Listening Below the Noise: A Meditation on the Practice of Silence* was sent to me by a circle of women (Peri Chickering, Barbara Cecil, Glennifer Gillespie, Dorian Baroni, and Beth Jandernoa) with the invitation to join in "an ongoing experiment to practice one day of Silence each month." This was not something that I needed to join, because I spend most mornings in solitude and know its value to my creativity and spirituality. When I was in my early forties, I was able to write because I woke up early and had two hours to myself before the household (then, a seven-year-old daughter, five-year-old son, dog, and husband) awoke and the morning hustle and bustle began. Since then, introvert that I am, I often think of solitude as delicious.

An example of the value of silence on creativity comes through LeClaire's description (2009, p. 138) of Kathleen Norris's exercise for elementary school children, which Kathleen Norris included in her book *Amazing Grace*. Norris told them that when she raised her hand, they could make all the noise they wanted to, and when she lowered her hand, they had to stop. The rules for silence were equally simple. When she raised her hand, they had to sit and make no noise at all. Then they were to write about both experiences. What she found was that making noise resulted in very little originality, while making silence liberated the imagination in so many of the children. I found myself intrigued by the tree images: one boy came up with "as slow and silent as a tree." Another wrote that "silence is a tree spreading its branches to the sun."

In the shelter and quiet of a tree that is a special place for a child or an adult, trees provide a sacred space or sanctuary. Under the canopy of branches and leaves, sunlight diffuses into dapples, provides shade when the sun is high and hot, and is an umbrella from the rain. In the shelter of a tree, we are aware of what is above us. In my mind's eye, I'm also now aware of an invisible branching root system under the visible tree, which spreads downward and outward in the earth, like a nest under us. We are cradled under trees. When we sit under a tree and lose track of time, we enter a soulful space in ourselves, induced by just being there. Fertile ideas can grow when there is time and space to brood on them. This brooding space serves as an incubator for insights and images. Might this have been why the Buddha became enlightened under a tree?

Siddhartha Gautama, the Buddha, and the Bodhi Tree

The man we know of as the Buddha was born in Nepal about 560 BCE and died about 480 BCE. His name was Siddhartha Gautama. His given name, Siddhartha, means "one who has accomplished his aim"; Gautama was his family name. "Buddha" means the enlightened one. According to the historical and legendary stories we have about him, he was the son of a king, whose mother died shortly after he was born. Upon his birth, astrologers saw two possible directions his life could take and said that, on reaching manhood, Siddhartha would either become a monk and an enlightened being or he would become a great king who would rule the world. The king asked what might cause Siddhartha to become a monk—in order to avoid this possibility. The astrologers replied, that it would result from meeting "a decrepit old man, a diseased man, a dead man, and a monk." Wanting his son to become the monarch, the king raised him in luxury and indulgence behind the walls of his palace. Siddhartha grew to manhood, married at sixteen, as was arranged, and had a son, all the while knowing nothing of life outside the guarded walls of wealth and privilege. Siddhartha's father, like so many other ambitious men who raise sons to carry out their hopes and ambitions, thought he could shape who his son would become.

And then one day, Prince Siddhartha ventured out with one servant to see how ordinary people lived. He went into a town and saw a decrepit old man, a sick man, and a corpse and he was shocked. He realized that everyone, including himself, was mortal and would grow old, suffer, and die. He became obsessed by his fears of growing old, of suffering and death, which now made it impossible to enjoy the luxuries and comforts he had. Then he met a monk who impressed him with his serenity, and decided to renounce the material world, which no longer gave him any satisfaction. He was twenty-nine when he set out on his quest to find answers to the mortal reality of aging, sickness, and death.

First he sought out Brahmin teachers and sages; then with five companions he became a yogi and practiced extreme deprivation, a follower of the ascetic path of denial of the body as a means of spiritual enlightenment. He had gone from the excesses of luxury to starvation, and had become emaciated and weak. When he decided that renunciation and mortification of the body did not provide answers but hastened the deterioration of body and mind, he had spent six years as a seeker. He left the forest where he had to forage for food, entered the outskirts of the city of Gaya, and there he sat under a huge tree. When he accepted food from a woman, he was abandoned by his five companions, who saw this middle way between indulgence and deprivation as unworthy. Sitting under this tree is where and when Siddhartha became enlightened. The tree is important in his story. It is referred to as the Bodhi tree or the Bo tree.

In Moyra Caldecott's *Myths of the Sacred Tree,* she tells how he sat under the great tree at Bohd Gaya for forty-nine days and was enlightened through the tree itself. She wrote:

> He could feel the great tree drawing nourishment and energy from the earth. He could feel it drawing nourishment and energy from the air and the sun. He began to feel the same energy pumping in his heart. He began to feel that there was no distinction between the tree and himself. He was the tree. The tree was him. The earth and the sky were also part of the tree and hence of him.

When his companions came that way again, they
found him so shining and radiant they could hardly
look at him directly.

"What has happened?" they asked.

But he did not reply.

He took a leaf from the tree and looked at it. In it was
the whole essence of the tree. In it was the essence of
the universe. . . . They saw it glowing with the same
radiance that he saw. (1933, p. 38)

In this imaginative story of the Buddha, when the companions looked at him after his enlightenment, they could see or
feel it in his serenity or through the subtle energy that we pick
up from one another. He was transformed, but had no words
for it. This story of Siddhartha's experience has, for me, a ring
of psychological authenticity—speculative as it is. Once he
had witnessed disease, aging, and death, these thoughts and
images intruded on his psyche, so that he could no longer
enjoy the life he had. People who suffer from obsessive intru-
sive thoughts are tormented and seek relief from the anxiety and depression that usually accompany such thoughts.
The ascetic path is one that shifts the compulsive focus to
controlling the body, but, like anorexia, offers no real relief.
Siddhartha's middle way brought him back to community
where he could accept food, and where under the Bodhi tree,
he had a transformative experience. The story that Caldecott
tells—that the tree gave him a deep sense of being part of all
that is—would be a deeply comforting illumination.

After his enlightenment, some say that he sat cross-
legged under this tree for seven days, and then moved to

sit under two other Bo trees in the same position for the same number of days. (In other versions, he sat under seven varieties of trees for forty-nine days.) This time of meditation and reflection makes psychological sense to anyone for whom the meaning of a mystical experience or an awesome archetypal image in a dream or vision is as significant as the revelation itself. For the Buddha, as for C. G. Jung, and the Jungian analysts whose calling it is to work in this soul realm, the work of enlightenment is more than the experience itself; it is the deep insight that comes from asking, "What is the meaning of this experience?" What have I learned and what can I take of it to others? For Jung it was a series of visions and active imagination that were revelations about the psyche and the collective unconscious, which he described and painted in *The Red Book*. When this inquiry brings insight into what helped and healed, for many people the impulse or new direction is then to take what is learned into the world to help others. Buddha's reflection on his enlightenment under the Bodhi tree led to his concepts of the Four Noble Truths and the Eightfold Way, the basis of Buddhism. He was thirty-five years old when he began traveling and teaching what he had learned, which he continued to do until he died at age eighty.

The Bodhi Tree

The Bodhi tree, or Bo tree, is called this because *bodhi* means being awake, enlightened, having supreme knowledge. It is not necessarily a particular tree, but the particular tree under which Siddhartha Gautama became the Buddha was most likely an Asiatic fig, botanically known as *Ficus religiosa,* which is called a pipal tree or the sacred fig tree in India. These trees are notable for their great size and longevity. The tree under which Siddhartha became enlightened was at Gaya, now called Bodh Gaya, around which a large monastic settlement formed. The main monastery is the Mahabodhi Temple, which became a UNESCO World Heritage Site in 2002. Bodh Gaya is the most important pilgrimage site for Buddhists.

The first scriptural reference to the Bodhi tree being established as an object of Buddhist worship is in the *Kalingabodhi Jataka*. A man who was the donor of the Jetavana monastery where the Buddha was living at the time asked if there was a place or object of reverence where devotees could pay their respects and offer homage when the Buddha was away. The Buddha said that the Bodhi tree was such a thing and a seed of the original tree was brought. A Bodhi tree (maybe the original one) can still be seen on the site of the old monastery at modern Sahet Hahet (Savatthi) in India.

The earliest records on the tree at Bodh Gaya are in the *Kalingabodhi Jataka*, which gives a vivid description of the tree and the surrounding area prior to the enlightenment, and the *Asokavadana*, which relates the story of King Ashoka's (third century BCE) conversion to Buddhism. His subsequent worship under the sacred tree apparently angered his queen to the point where she ordered the tree to be felled. Ashoka then piled up earth around the stump and poured milk on its roots. The tree miraculously revived and grew to a height of 37 meters (over 121 feet) He then surrounded the tree with a stone wall some three meters high for its protection. Ashoka's daughter Sangamitta, a Buddhist nun, took a shoot of the tree to Sri Lanka where

King Devanampiyatissa planted it at the Mahavihara monastery in Anuradhapura about 245 BCE. It still flourishes today and is the oldest continually documented tree in the world.

In 600 CE, King Sesanka, a zealous Shiavite, again destroyed the tree at Bodh Gaya. The event was recorded by Hiuen T'sang, along with the planting of a new Bodhi tree sapling by King Purnavarma in 620 CE. At this time, during the annual celebration of Vesak, thousands of people from all over India would gather to anoint the roots of the holy tree with perfumed water and scented milk, and to offer flowers and music. Hiuen T'sang wrote: "The tree stands inside a fort like structure surrounded on the south, west and north by a brick wall. It has pointed leaves of a bright green colour. Having opened a door, one could see a large trench in the shape of a basin. Devotees worship with curd, milk and perfumes such as sandalwood, camphor and so on."

Much later, the English archeologist Alexander Cunningham recorded: "In 1862 I found this tree very much decayed; one large stem to the westward with three branches was still green, but the other branches were barkless and rotten. I next saw the tree in 1871 and again in 1875, when it had become completely decayed, and shortly afterwards in 1876 the only remaining portion of the tree fell over the west wall during a storm, and the old pipal tree was gone. Many seeds, however, had been collected and the young scion of the parent tree were already in existence to take its place." The present Bodhi tree is most probably the fourth descendant of that original tree to be planted at this site. The Bodhi tree plays a very important role for Buddhists of all traditions, being a reminder and an inspiration, a symbol of peace, of Buddha's enlightenment and of the ultimate potential that lies within us all. (Buddha Mind).

The Leaf

In the midst of writing this chapter, I went to Houston, Texas, to speak on the subject of "Turning Points: Creativity and the Mystery of Healing." The design on the program and on the invitations to this dinner event was one standing leaf. When I saw it, I recalled that this was the symbol of Buddha's enlightenment in Caldecott's story. The awed response to seeing it reminded me of the similar response from the initiates of the Eleusinian Mysteries of ancient Greece when, at the very end of the initiation, a single sheaf of wheat was revealed.

The word "mystery" is derived from the Greek *mystes*, which was the name for the initiate and is the source of the word "mystic." When indigenous North American peoples translate their spirituality into English, they often speak of it as "the Great Mystery." In common use, anything uncanny that cannot be explained logically is a mystery. In fiction, a mystery book is about solving a murder. Death is the ultimate human mystery, one that engrossed Siddhartha in his quest for enlightenment. Revelation or illumination of the "mystery" was embodied and symbolized by the leaf and the sheaf. In my talk, I spoke of mystery as related to that uniquely human sense of having a soul and thereby being drawn to the numinous, which is a perception that connects us to a divine, invisible world and to what is immortal in us.

At this event, the Jung Center of Houston was honoring the Children's Cancer Center, where the possibility of death accompanies every diagnosis. In working with cancer patients and writing *Close to the Bone: Life-Threatening Illness as a Soul Journey,* I had often heard from women with breast cancer that "cancer was the worst thing that had ever happened to them, and the best thing." Meaning that the cancer diagnosis became the turning point in their lives. In the descent into the metaphoric underworld, there is the fear of death; the effects of surgery, radiation, and chemotherapy; the unsought changes in themselves; and the response of others to them. In that cancer patients face the possibility of not returning back to life, they can identify with Persephone, the goddess who was abducted by Hades into the underworld, which is the mythic basis of the Eleusinian Mysteries as told in *The Homeric Hymn to Demeter,* which tells that the initiate was blessed and now would no longer fear death.

The Eleusinian Mysteries were the most sacred and important religious rituals of ancient Greece for over two thousand years, until the sanctuary was destroyed by the invading Goths in the fifth century. The "secrets" were not to be told and, apparently, never were revealed. People are not good at keeping secrets, which makes it unlikely that these secrets could be revealed in words. I speculate that the initiates entered an altered state of ecstatic consciousness induced by a combination of expectation, ritual, darkness, sound, and possibly a hallucinogenic drink. We do know of the procession and ritual at the sea that preceded entering the sanctuary grounds, and of a great shout and a blaze of light that could be seen from outside. The initiate was transformed by the experience. The sheaf of wheat held up at the end of the Eleusinian Mysteries, like Buddha's leaf, must have been a wordless transmission, a numinous symbol imbued with meaning (Kerenyi, *Eleusis,* 1967). The dread of death was overcome. Similarly, once Siddhartha was enlightened, he no longer was obsessed with his fears of disease, old age, and death.

Christianity is the mystery religion that supplanted the Eleusinian Mysteries, in that the basis of the Christian experience is also mystical and personal. The person who is saved, converted, born-again, transformed, or baptized in the spirit, who experiences *metanoia,* can share the experience of Jesus Christ, who was crucified, died, put in a tomb, and overcame death: just as the initiate into the Eleusinian Mysteries must have identified with the divine daughter, Persephone, who was taken into the realm of death and returned every spring. The mystery religions including Christianity have rituals in which the initiates receive an experience that changes them and overcome a fear of death. Life can also give the same message to people who are present at the moment someone dies.

Presence When the Soul Passes

Women are the caretakers of the dying and are likely those who are present when a person dies. This is so when death occurs at home, but also in hospitals, where those that are with the dying and who may witness the end are family members and nurses. To be present when someone dies is to be in attendance when a soul leaves the body. Death is extraordinary and ordinary, a natural passing from one stage to the next. Men as a gender, especially those who have control issues and are focused on acquiring power or admiration, either as the patient or the doctor, face death as a fight to the last breath. How we budget medical care is upside down in its priorities as a result, with astronomical costs paid toward the end of life for hospitalizations, heroic measures, state-of-the-art technology, and life support. Women who are caretakers of others through every stage of life would rather money were spent on preventing disease, treating illnesses, and enhancing the quality of health and life.

I was present at the exact moment when my father died. He had been sent home to die, after surgery, radiation, and che-motherapy could do no more. I was a first-year resident in psychiatry and had taken a leave of absence to be with my parents at this time. His eyes were open and he looked at something I could not see. I saw his eyes widen and his face became infused with joy, and then he was gone. That look was a gift to me. His face told me that he was going toward something that was wonderful, that he was not afraid—so that I needn't be. He was gone in a heartbeat or a nanosecond. One moment he was there, and then he was really gone, leaving behind a worn-out body that was no more him than old clothes he had once worn. When I have brought this up in my lectures, invariably, others come forth with similar stories. I might add here that, sometimes in coma, people who are dying moan as if in pain—or labor. Women who are midwives of newborns and of the soul at the time of death, those whose archetype is Hecate, the goddess of the crossroad whose time is twilight, know such things just as they know the stages of labor. At the end, even when the last stages were difficult, those who have been privileged to be present at the moment that the soul leaves the body, and able to perceive such things, comment on the deep sense of peace they felt, and often also of sensing a number of spirits in the room.

The World Soul (Anima Mundi)

That there is an underlying sacred pattern and wholeness in the universe to which we and all things are a part is the basis of indigenous spirituality as well as Eastern mysticism; it's the soulful element in Celtic spirituality. It is soul in us that perceives that matter is held by or imbued with soul and part of the *anima mundi,* or world soul. Within this vision, everything in nature is sacred. I would add, seen also as beautiful or awesome, and sometimes even deeply sweet.

People who perceive soulfulness in trees have experiences and beliefs similar to all indigenous people who feel themselves related to the spirit world that inhabits all living things.

The perception I had at the moment of my father's death gives me a deep appreciation of the analogy that Plato drew about the *anima mundi.* He conceived of the world soul as animating the world in the same way as the soul animates the human body. In *Timaeus,* he wrote: "Therefore, we may consequently state that: this world is indeed a living being endowed with a soul and intelligence . . . a single visible living entity containing all other living entities, which by their nature are all related."

Bodhisattvas

I had heard the term *bodhisattva* used in reference to the Dalai Lama and to Buddha. I took this to mean an enlightened being who could have left the wheel of existence, and out of compassion chose to help others attain enlightenment. This definition and these two examples made a bodhisattva far from an ordinary human being and, from a Western perspective, esoteric besides. But in Houston, as I thought about Buddha's leaf and was preparing to speak about Turning Points for people with cancer, the concept in my mind broadened liberally to include lots of ordinary people. I thought about women who volunteer at breast cancer diagnostic centers, for example, who know what the cancer journey is like, including the discomfort of the tests and the apprehension and fear, who are there to make it easier for others. I recalled Lawrence LeShan's work with terminal cancer patients, which led to their remissions and his conviction that remission and giving back are related. I thought about the concept of the "wounded healer" whose compassion to help and a deep understanding began with personal, usually early suffering that led to entering a helping profession. (Siddhartha could fit this definition when he became the Buddha.)

I now see "ordinary bodhisattvas" wherever I find people motivated to help others. At the United Nations, many of the non-governmental organizations (NGOs) represented at the meetings of the Commission on the Status of Women were founded and then staffed by women who themselves survived being trafficked or oppressed in the many ways there are to abuse or misuse or neglect, which people with power can inflict on vulnerable individuals and groups. At the last meeting, a young American woman spoke of having been trafficked into a brothel and of the importance of raising awareness that this happens to American girls, and those who know what this life is like and have made their way back can help others. I see bodhisattvas in the musicians, visionaries, authors, and artists whose work was informed by their suffering, and who, after their suffering was redeemed through their creativity, took that one step further to help others. Standing behind many nonprofits are these ordinary bodhisattvas—individuals who are survivors who want to give back by helping others. They are also people whose empathy enlightened them to the suffering of others, and what they are now doing is their creative and compassionate response. An ordinary bodhisattva is, as I am describing, a person in touch with the archetype of the bodhisattva, who acts from this deep place of compassion. They are not saints or perfect beings, but when they do whatever they do to alleviate suffering and help others, they are doing soul work. I think that seeing ourselves and others in this light adds an awareness of and appreciation for the good that is done and the goodness in people.

The Tao and the Girl Scout

Every summer, beginning when I was about nine, I went to Girl Scout Camp near Big Bear Lake in Southern California. It was a rustic camp and we slept in sleeping bags out of doors. Around us were tents to hold our belongings and a few Jeffrey pine trees with bark that had a sweet scent of vanilla. We went to sleep under the Milky Way. I remember how beautiful the nighttime sky was overhead and how immense. Sometimes we focused our vision on the starry sky above us, with the hope of seeing a shooting star—the occasional comet or meteor that left a streak of light in its wake—in order to make a wish. One summer—I think I was ten—I was looking up at the stars, when a shift of perception happened in me. In a moment of insight, I *knew* that I was part of this awesome, beautiful universe. "What my eyes saw, my soul experienced. I felt a sense of reverence and awe at the boundlessness and beauty of the universe. It touched me. I felt God's presence in the mountains, trees, and immense sky. What was above me and around me and included me was unlimited, eternal and alive" (Bolen, *The Tao of Psychology*, 2004, p. 1). It was an initiation into the subjective reality of God or of the eternal Tao, an inner revelation, a shift out of the ordinary into a mystical, intuitive awareness.

Later I would realize that mine was an extrovert's perception of being related to everything in the universe, once I read Frederick Franck's introverted account, in *The Zen of Seeing: Seeing/Drawing as Meditation*:

> On a dark afternoon—I was ten or eleven—I was walking on a country road. On my left a patch of curly kale, on my right, some yellowed Brussels sprouts. I felt a snowflake on my cheek, and from far away in the charcoal gray sky, I saw the slow approach of a snow storm. I stood still.
>
> Some flakes were now falling around my feet. A few melted as they hit the ground. Others stayed intact. Then I heard the falling of the snow, with the softest hissing sound.
>
> I stood transfixed, listening . . . and knew what can never be expressed: that the natural is supernatural, and that I am the eye that hears and the ear that sees.

And what is outside happens in me, that outside and inside are unseparated (1973, p. 114).

Franck's poetic description seems to need explanation, since several manuscript readers questioned whether the "eye that hears" and "ear that sees" was a transposed mistake, which it is not. In the mystical moment of gnosis, reality may be intensely perceived simultaneously with an illumination about reality—and grasped in its entirety. I would say by the soul, by "I," rather than by ears or eyes.

What I perceived in my moment of insight as a child stayed with me. I hadn't a word for the concept of underlying oneness until much later and didn't make the connection until I began writing a book about synchronicity that became *The Tao of Psychology: Synchronicity and the Self.* C. G. Jung coined the term "synchronicity" to describe the phenomenon of meaningful coincidences. I had given a lecture on the synchronicity and because of a series of unlikely—synchronistic—events, Marie Cantlon, an editor at Harper & Row, had asked if I might be interested in writing a book on the subject. Of course, it was flattering, but having a young family and a part-time psychiatric practice, I simply could not imagine when I might write. A couple of years later, when I longed to have some time for myself, I began wondering if Marie would remember and still be interested. It was on my hesitant mind when my answering service gave me a message to return a call to a former patient who I thought had left the area permanently. When I called the number she had left, an operator answered, "This is Harper & Row." This was one of several synchronicities that led me to become an author.

The Tao of Psychology

I was absorbed in thinking about synchronicity when I had an intuition about the relationship between the Tao and the Self. (In Jungian psychology, the Self is the archetype of meaning that can be used interchangeably with divinity.) The Tao in Eastern thought holds that everything that we can perceive with our senses is one of "the ten thousand things," manifestations of the invisible oneness to which everything relates. This unifying principle underlies the major Eastern religions: Hinduism, Buddhism, Confucianism, and Taoism. It was a purely intellectual aha! until I remembered the sudden, meaningful shift in perception out under the stars in summer camp, and how it is possible to know something at the soul level, or in our bones, which is far different from the idea. It is an inner certainty.

The sudden shift of perception from separateness to being part of nature or the universe isn't scary or disorienting. It often begins with an attitude of wonder, followed by pleasure, appreciation, and joy of this moment. It is an openhearted child response in a child or adult. Too many people become disillusioned or even cynical as children, especially without access and exposure to nature. For those who can see, nature is an unending source of wonder. There is a growing concern that urban children are suffering from "nature-deficit disorder," and alienated from nature. One major consequence is the loss of a sense of wonder, which nature—in her abundance and beauty and wildness—draws from us.

Apollo 14 Astronaut Edgar Mitchell was trained as a scientist and an engineer. In 1971, he walked on the moon and was returning to Earth from space when he had an experience that changed his life. As he approached Earth, he had an epiphany, which he described as an "ecstasy of unity." He was filled with an inner conviction; he knew that the beautiful blue world he was returning to was part of a living system, harmonious and whole, a "universe of consciousness" in which we all participate. This experience changed him and the direction of his life. After he landed, he spent the next several months rigorously studying mystical writing from Eastern and Western spiritual traditions. He found a Sanskrit description of *savikalpa samadhi* that he believed fit his experience: a moment in which an individual recognizes the separateness of all things yet understands that the separateness is but an illusion (McNeill, "Edgar Mitchell," *Shift*, November 2006).

Two years later, Mitchell founded the Institute of Noetic Sciences (IONS). The word "noetic" comes from the ancient Greek *nous*, for which there is no exact equivalent in English. It refers to "inner knowing," a kind of intuitive consciousness—direct and immediate access to knowledge beyond what is available to our normal senses and the power of reason (IONS).

The World of Nature as Tonic for the Soul

In *Letters from a Wild State: Rediscovering Our True Relationship to Nature*, author James G. Cowan describes his journey into the visionary realms where sages and traditional peoples are at home. Through the friendship of Aboriginal tribesmen in Australia, Cowan entered their mystical world. He writes:

> We should never forget how important the wild world of nature is as a tonic to the soul. Religious

doctrine may give form to the great metaphors, the myths and rites that govern our lives. It may grant us mystical insight by way of ascetic disciplines. . . . It may even lead us along paths of spiritual enlightenment whereby we personally attain a deeper sense of well-being, even bliss. But it is to the earth upon which we walk that we should occasionally look if we are to preserve our intellectual and spiritual heritage. If we destroy this because of our insensitivity to it as a metaphysical environment, we are in danger of destroying ourselves. This is the great lesson all traditional peoples can teach us: how to protect who we are by protecting what made us (1991, pp. xiii–xiv).

What they feel in the earth, what they hear in the trees are the primordial whispers emanating from an ancient source. . . . It may be said of these people that they continually feel the need of what does not exist (p. 8).

Cowan attributes this yearning to awe. "These nomads are able to lift up the mystery in themselves toward the mystery in the universe. They are able to perceive in themselves something equal to what is beyond them" (p. 9).

Bron Taylor, professor of religion at the University of Florida and author of *Dark Green Religion*, notes that people are turning to Mother Earth to fill a spiritual void and that large numbers of people in Europe and the United States express a trust in nature as inherently spiritual or sacred. The Catholic Church was reportedly offended by the green spirituality of James Cameron's *Avatar*, with its message of hope and faith in the interconnectedness of life, and chastised the filmmaker for presenting nature as "a divinity to worship" and for promoting "all those pseudo-doctrines that turn ecology into the religion of the millennium" (Barton, "Eco-Spirituality," *Globe and Mail*, January 25, 2010).

Nature Speaks

Linda Milks began the Nature Speaks Project after she pulled over to the side of the road in response to the "all points bulletin" she sensed coming from the trees. She is building an online database of interviews with people who communicate with trees (*www.naturespeaks.org*). I suspect that this is not as unusual as it may seem. One of my hopes for this book is that my words will help others to claim their own soul connections with nature and trees.

In her interview, Charlie Toledo, an indigenous wise-woman elder, descendent of the Towa tribe, native to New Mexico, said she asked kids how they would commune with trees, and they knew—just "go and be quiet by a tree." (I wonder, do kids come into the world knowing such things—and then forget?)

Charlie commented:

> That's how you would start with the tree—come and breathe with your back to the tree. And then wait until you can really feel the life force of the tree. That's the first thing, to feel that in your body, then you begin to get it. I often say the best meditation teacher you'll ever have is a tree. Once you connect with the tree ask it to take your grounding cord down with it. . . . But then the essence of meditation is your

breath. So you breathe in and out with the tree and get that circle of energy going with your breath. You do that for a couple hours a day for a couple weeks. Because I think people think, oh I'm going to talk to nature, I'll just go out and start chatting away . . . and it's like no, you have to take the time to make the connection ("Charlie Toledo Interview," Nature Speaks Project, 2005).

Charlie Toledo's explanation of how to do this requires making a rather large commitment; for busy Americans, "a couple of hours a day for a couple of weeks" is a lot of time. To begin a spiritual practice of meditation is a similar commitment, though some take to it immediately. Maybe like other relationships with people or animals, there are trees with which there is an almost instant rapport in the same way as happens between people. In her interview with Linda Milks, Meg Beeler, a shamanic teacher in Sonoma, California, said that she would see a tree and make a beeline for it because it had such a strong pull on her. She wanted to spend time to be with trees that draw her to them. But then, she didn't know what else to do. Now she knows how to "exchange energy with trees." At Linda's request during the interview, she went outside and found a blue oak tree and described the process: "I walked around the tree and greeted it and asked permission to exchange energy with it. I put my hands on the tree and blew into it as a means of connecting. Since the exchange of energy is back to back, I put my back to the tree and opened to what it had to tell me and opened my energy to the tree" ("Meg Beeler Interview," Nature Speaks Project, 2008).

In the article "Connecting with the Web: Begin with One Tree," Meg Beeler wrote that it isn't hard to make a connection with a tree:

Everyone has a special tree somewhere. When shape or size or color draw our attention, the tree seems to call us, offering us the possibility of deeper connections. Our bodies remember the childhood trees we climbed or read under, swung from or used for imaginary games. So it is not hard—we only have to drop our adult self-consciousness and judgment— to make relationships with the trees we are drawn to. That might mean leaning up against an ancient oak during a hike, or lying along the low branch of one. It might mean circling the biggest tree in our neighborhood, letting fingertips draw across bark daily to say hello. Or it might mean painting the tree or imprinting its bark into clay.

In an experiment that opens my heart with wonder each time I think of it, experienced meditators sat with their backs to trees and entered a meditative state. Concurrently, using highly sensitive recording devices, Bernie Krause and his cohorts measured the rhythms of human breath and tree sap rising and falling. Guess what? Each tree slowed the flow of its sap to match the breathing pattern of its meditator! *The trees consciously entrained with the humans.* This means that we humans can teach ourselves to entrain with a tree by letting our breath, our consciousness, and our awareness match the tree's awareness, and by listening to the tree's story, advice, and requests (*Shifting Consciousness News,* August 2006).

Note: Bernie Krause is an American bioacoustician, who coined the word "biophony." Krause holds a PhD in bioacoustics from Union Institute of Cincinnati. Prior to this, he was a noted musician as a member of The Weavers. He and Paul Beaver introduced the synthesizer to pop music and film, and he is credited with making contributions to the beginning of both the New Age and electronica musical movements.

Living in a Sacred World

Often our deepest subjective experiences become minimized, ridiculed, or pathologized when they are processed by left-brained authority. Anything that is intuitively grasped but cannot be proven scientifically is discounted. In the case of parapsychological research, however, it hasn't mattered much how rigorous and up to standards it is, when minds cannot accept the premise of spiritual or psychic experience because it is beyond left-brain comprehension. Left-brain logic is the "either-or" part of the brain, which cannot seem to grasp and hold two apparent truths without choosing one over the other, or making one right and one wrong, or one superior and the other inferior. Left-brain vision measures; it is used to judge and assess. There is subject and object, I and it. To see with "soft eyes" is looking through a different lens. "Soft eyes" are receptive and accepting. These are the eyes that are like open windows to the soul, eyes that are unguarded and can be looked into to perceive the soul.

It is through them that we see the soulfulness in the world around us, and it is through the heart center that we behold what we see in our body-psyche. Soul recognizes soul and is nourished by it. Soul feels invisible connections and it is this that draws tree people to trees.

Thich Nhat Hanh: We Are Trees

Thich Nhat Hanh, Buddhist monk, poet, author, and peace activist, was exiled from Vietnam in 1973, after he headed the Vietnamese Buddhist Peace Delegation to the Paris Peace Accords. In "The Last Tree" in *Dharma Gaia*, he describes what he would do when he visited a new place and was homesick:

> I knew I could go outside, in the backyard or to a park, and find a place to practice breathing and smiling under the trees.
>
> I know that in our previous life we were trees, and even in this life we continue to be trees. Without trees, we cannot have people, therefore trees and people inter-are. We *are* trees, and air, bushes, and clouds. If trees cannot survive, humankind is not going to survive either. We get sick because we have damaged our own environment, and we are in mental anguish because we are so far away from our true mother, Mother Nature (1990, p. 218).

7

WISE LIKE A TREE: TREE PEOPLE

On the very edge of a steep hillside path in Muir Woods, there is an old growth redwood tree with an opening from the path into the base of the trunk. I see that there is a dry dirt floor and I step in. Inside, the ceiling is considerably higher; it is a spacious space for one person. The space is here because the tree was once on fire and this was a deep burn around which the living tree continued to grow. This space is in an old growth redwood that may have lived here for over a thousand years. Inside this tree, the most natural response is to be still and just be—a human being inside a tree being. A thought came to mind, "Wise like a tree."

Musings on "Wise Like a Tree"

This particular old growth redwood is one tree among many, some as old, some older, some younger. There are many others in this forest that have black scars from a long-ago fire or fire-created cave-like spaces in them, some quite large in even larger trees on the floor of the park. The last known big fire was over two hundred years ago. The idea "wise like a tree" came from or into a stillness in me. I had been walking along a trail and paying attention so I wouldn't trip or slip, as well as noticing what was around me. My mind was not working on this book. Once I was inside the tree, my attention was held by it. I stood still. Did the tree communicate to me or did the thought occur to me? I think the latter was the case. Insights, answers, and solutions come to me when a creative and meaningful project is in the back of my mind. It is possible, however, that these words came from the tree. I can accept the notion that trees "talk to" people, because I talk to people who have such "conversations." Intuitive or psychic gardeners seem to be doing something similar. Betty Karr, my administrative assistant and a Millionth Circle convener, had an "of course" response when I brought the subject up. Her property in Indiana included many acres of woodlands. She would notice when one of the trees "seemed sad." She could tune into the tree, and invariably what the problem was and what she should do would come into her mind. Often the answer that came was outside her own awareness, such as the infestation of beetles too high up in the tree for her to have seen. At home, when one of her houseplants is "unhappy," she will find out what it needs: usually their needs are more predictable, more water, less water, a change of potting mix, moving it to get more light or less. Betty may pick up that a plant is "unhappy" or "sad" before the houseplant looks like something is wrong. I think it is that subtle, tuned-into-others receptivity that is often called female intuition.

When plants, trees, animals, or people thrive under someone's care, invariably that person with a "green thumb," or the "horse whisperer" or the doctor with a healing touch, or the psychotherapist whose people do well has love for the individuals (from plant to person) and a love for the work. There is a respect for and a recognition of the "other"—a relationship exists. This is about love and soul, the subtle, huge field of energy that healing and gnosis taps into, which should be paid attention to and not dismissed. Just imagine what science and modern medicine *and* the subtle energies of love and soul could do together!

Women Are Wise Like a Tree

As I learned how trees simultaneously do a great many different things, and how every tree is part of an ecological system, I saw that women's multitasking could be described as like a tree, and how most women are also in a complex ecological system of relationships. Multitasking is what most women do. They keep track of children and other people in their lives, think about the meals to prepare (from what and for whom), keep a mental or written shopping list, and see that clothes are cleaned or in need of repair. Most have a work life as well as a home life, and so also have responsibilities and time to account for. Add to this volunteer activities and causes, invitations to respond to, and events to attend. Multitasking is helped by the number of fibers (which make up the corpus callosum) connecting the left brain to the right brain and are required to shift focus, which involves going back and forth from logic to feeling, from being in the moment and then aware of being on a schedule, even from seeing in pictures to descriptive words.

Almost everything that women do involves working cooperatively with other people, which develops with practice. It helps to have the ability to read faces and hear the tone in a voice, and remember past emotional histories with people. These specific abilities are talents women as a gender have because of female brain circuitry, hormonal physiology, and in most circumstances because they have learned to pay attention to men's moods and unexpressed feelings. Babies teach their mothers and caretakers to pay attention to subtle signs as well as loud cries of distress. Paying attention to the needs of another is usually women's work.

The Female Brain and The Male Brain

With the development of highly technical tools such as positron emission tomography (PET) scans and functional magnetic resonance imaging (ƒMRI), researchers can see inside the brain in real time and under a variety and range of functioning. Neurochemistry now can measure hormones and how they fluctuate under different circumstances. As a result, neuroscience can now tell us about the differences between the female brain and the male brain, and why at this crucial time, women have qualities that humanity and the planet need. Louann Brizendine, MD, at the University of California San Francisco Medical Center conducted an exhaustive review of brain research and made this new science accessible in her two recent books, *The Female Brain* and *The Male Brain*. Brizendine summarizes brain development and the differences between male and female brains, noting also brain development and changes that occur through stages of life from the fetus in the uterus to late adulthood. As I read and digested the information, what kept emerging in my thoughts is how much hard science information supports the need for women to become a force for transformative change because of innate talents and abilities.

In *f*MRI scans of areas that process experience, there are significant differences between female and male brains. Women's brain centers for language and hearing have 11 percent more neurons than men's do. The center of emotion and memory formation (hippocampus) is also larger, as are the brain circuits for language and observing emotions in others. This means that women are, on average, better at expressing emotions and remembering the details of emotional events as well as being better at knowing how others are responding or feeling. The area of the brain that weighs options in making decisions (anterior cingulate cortex) is larger in women than in men, as is the part of the brain that inhibits aggression (prefrontal cortex). The part of the brain that processes sensations in the body related to picking up emotional data (the insula) is also larger in the female brain. Overall, the female brain is geared toward assessing the feelings and intentions of others, engaging in communication, and defusing conflict.

By contrast, men have two and a half times more brain space devoted to sex, and the center that registers fear and triggers aggression (amygdala) and alerts the brain to danger is larger than in female brains. Since women use both sides of the brain more than men do, it wasn't surprising to learn that women's brains are symmetrical, while there is an anatomical asymmetry in the size of the two hemispheres in heterosexual men (Brizendine, *The Male Brain*, 2010, p. 134).

At the World Economic Summit in Davos, Switzerland, in 2009, there was serious discussion that if it had been Lehman Brothers & Sisters, instead of Lehman Brothers, the failure of this company that was a key element in the worldwide crisis might not have happened. Risk-taking competitive men created the situation that led to the market collapse and financial crisis. Men are motivated by their need to maintain status and territory; when either is threatened, there is an increase in testosterone and cortisol, which activate the emotional center of fear, anger, and aggression in the brain (amygdala). The brain circuits of high-testosterone men lead them to dominate other males and establish hierarchy. There is an instinctive response to protect their turf, with anger, aggression, and risk-taking driven by hormones.

Male brain dominance in a global world means that decisions that affect everyone and the environment are made by high-testosterone men driven to dominate and win. This results in ongoing political, military, and economic conflicts which cause collateral damage—especially to women and children. Gender balance through empowerment and equality of women would make use of the female brain and the oxytocin response to further collaboration and defuse conflict wherever decisions are made.

Women and Concern for the Planet

Networks of women are responding to the planet's life-support crisis before it's too late. What women are doing about climate change, water scarcity, drilling for oil, toxic contamination, stewardship of space, and deforestation was reported in a survey article in *World Pulse: Global Issues Through the Eyes of Women*, related through the stories of individual women. For example, the story about the work of Edina Yahana, Tanzania's first woman village forester, begins with an overview about women's tree wisdom and activism: "Women have long been defenders of our forests. They've recognized that when forests fall, the livelihoods of local communities fall with them. Animals flee, soil quality thins, floods and landslides increase, and carbon-sequestering canopies are lost. Whether planting new trees or starting sustainable economic endeavors, women are regenerating the 'lungs of the Earth'" (*World Pulse*, 2010, pp. 32–33).

Edina walks from village to village, and says of her work: "It is important to me to spread the message of conservation. These forests have been here much longer than any of us, and they can't protect themselves." When she gets to a village, Edina teaches a wide variety of subjects—about butterfly farming and beekeeping, techniques to make houses out of bricks instead of lumber, how to make fuel-efficient stoves to reduce gathering of firewood, and to plant trees. Like trees, women are involved in a wide variety of activities with the earth, air, and life around them, and any subject touches on another, which broadens the conversation as they talk. They talk about the negative effect on the land of illegal timber harvesting and gold mining and the harm caused by the use of slash-and-burn techniques for farming. Meeting together, learning and sharing what they know and care about, village women become aware that others share their views or support their ideas. From this validation, there is support to speak up, which leads women to become involved in community decision making.

"Wise Like a Tree?" Endangered Trees and Endangered Women

I thought about tree wisdom: how trees are the heart of ecosystems where there is diversity of life, interdependency, and adaptation. I thought about how interdependency and adaptation occur naturally in and around any single stand-alone tree, as well as in groves. Trees are wise. They take and give back. They made life possible on Earth, and if we do not destroy our rain forests and arboreal forests, they will continue to absorb carbon and gases and make our planet's air breathable. They collaborate and have reciprocal relationships. Human beings are endangering themselves and the planet by failing to value what trees do, as well as value what they do for us. When trees are property, expendable, some with economic value, but otherwise of no intrinsic or spiritual value, they become endangered. This is true for an individual tree, such as the Monterey pine that no longer stands in front of my house. Many species of trees may be gone forever, such as the largest palm on Earth, extinct from Easter Island. The thousand-year-old redwoods I walk amidst are among the less than 3 percent that remain. According to the World Resources Institute, more than 80 percent of the Earth's natural forests have already been destroyed (*National Geographic*).

Like trees, in many places women and girls are considered property, devalued, and treated badly. Yet what women naturally do enhances the possibilities for peace and sustainability. Women are called the empathic gender because they can understand the feelings and needs of others; they react to stress differently than men do, with conversation and collaboration more likely wherever conflicts may arise. This is women's oxytocin "tend and befriend" response, while men's "fight or flight" testosterone-enhanced response makes peaceful resolutions more difficult.

Educate women and girls, and families benefit in many proven ways. Women will use resources more wisely and, as microcredit lenders know, can borrow, invest in their own small business efforts, and pay back the loan when men have not. In Haiti, after the earthquake, vouchers to receive bags of rice were given only to women. At first, vouchers were given to men as well, but this stopped when the men sold the rice and spent the money on themselves, while the women took the rice to feed their families.

Water and Women

Access to safe drinking water and basic sanitation is a problem for over one billion people. When none is available on the premises, collecting water is predominantly women's work. According to UN figures, 64 percent of all water collection is done by women, 25 percent by men, with children collecting 11 percent of water for households; of that 11 percent, 7 percent are girls, 4 percent boys. Although men and boys are stronger and water is heavy, it falls upon women and girls to do this. It is estimated that women and children in Africa alone spend forty billion hours every year fetching and carrying water, a figure equivalent to a year's labor for the entire workforce of France (Goetz, "Who Answers to Women?" UNIFEM, 2009, p. 37). Girls drop out of school in many rural areas because they have to walk for hours to collect water. Women and girls become potential prey for rape and harassment when they are unprotected and have to travel distances to fetch water. Wherever women have a say in village decisions, then water becomes a high priority.

Overall, the situation for women is not getting better, and yet the success stories are heartening. In the village of Nazlet Fargallah in Upper Egypt, women gathered water up to four times a day, using sewage-contaminated water for washing. Lacking latrines, they waited until dark to relieve themselves, leaving them ill and vulnerable to violence. The situation changed when a local government water and sanitation project introduced female health visitors and enabled women to participate in community and household decisions about how to improve health and livelihoods. The seven hundred households now have two taps and a latrine each. There is more awareness of the connection between sanitation and disease. Women spend less time collecting water and have gained dignity and security. Another successful effort made potable water available to indigenous Maasai families living in Emayia, Kenya, where girls had to fetch water before they came to school, and on missing morning lessons were told that they might as well stay at home. Now they have time to study and play.

Women's Equality and Empowerment

There is a hope and action moving through the world that would bring the heart and skills of girls and women to the planet at this time. Attending the forums, panels, and workshops offered by the non-governmental organizations affiliated with the UN Commission on the Status of Women has made me very aware of what is being done and could be done. If the Beijing Platform for Action that came out of the 4th UN World Conference on Women in 1995, which focused on making human rights women's rights, and women's rights human rights, and if the Millennium Development Goals (2000) were achieved, there would be a marked shift toward peace and sustainability. Once women are involved, priorities shift toward services that help people.

The year 2009 marked the 30th anniversary of the Convention on the Elimination of All Forms of Discrimination Against Women (CEDAW). It is the international bill of rights for women, and is used throughout the world to hold governments accountable in ensuring that women's rights are achieved in practice. The United States has not signed it—to our shame—though it now has sponsors in the Senate.

The Girl Effect

Research shows that powerful social and economic changes come about when girls have the opportunity to participate in their society. Adolescent girls are uniquely capable of raising the standard of living in the developing world. Girls are the most likely agents of change, but they are often invisible in their societies and to our media ("Girls Count," Center for Global Development, International Center for Research on Women and Population Council, 2008).

When a girl in the developing world receives seven or more years of education, she marries four years later and has 2.2 fewer children. An extra year of primary school boosts girls' eventual wages by 10 to 20 percent; an extra year of secondary school, by 15 to 25 percent. There is a consistent relationship between better infant and child health and higher levels of schooling among mothers. When women and girls earn income, they reinvest 90 percent of it in their families, as compared to only 30 to 40 percent by a man. More than one-quarter of the population in Asia, Latin America, the Caribbean, and sub-Saharan Africa are girls and young women aged ten to twenty-four. The total global population of girls in that age bracket is already the largest in history and is expected to peak in the next decade.

Meanwhile, approximately one-quarter of girls in developing countries are not in school. Of the world's 130 million out-of-school youth, 70 percent are girls. One out of seven marries before the age of fifteen, 38 percent marry before age eighteen. One-quarter to one-half of girls in developing countries become mothers before age eighteen, and fourteen million girls aged fifteen to nineteen give birth in developing countries each year. Medical complications from pregnancy are the leading cause of death among girls age fifteen to nineteen worldwide. Of fifteen- to twenty-four-year-olds living with HIV in Africa, 75 percent are female. In impoverished countries, lack of resources (and customs favoring educating boys) drives girls out of school and into early marriage, childbirth, and HIV infection. The results are irreversible for girls. Yet when girls are supported, educated, and empowered, their communities and countries benefit. Education is just the start. To make it work, a girl needs a safe environment, her identity secured with basic things like a birth certificate and skills. The Nike Foundation and NoVo Foundation are spending one hundred million dollars to fund Girl Effect programs.

In the discussions that led President Obama to send thirty thousand more troops to Afghanistan, the cost to maintain and support one soldier for one year, was *one million dollars.* This equals thirty billion dollars per year. Imagine the good that would ripple out if this amount were spent on the Girl Effect.

The Girl Effect is about breaking the cycle of poverty and building a sustainable global economy that can't happen until women and girls are included, especially when they are the solution. However, girls will say, "Changing my life requires changing his mind." Men as fathers, brothers, and teachers can step in at critical moments to support girls and women's opportunities or to block them. Changing attitudes of boys and men has to be part of the solution, which many NGOs are working on doing. The power men and boys assume they have over women and girls is a patriarchal pattern, perpetrated by violence and by not educating girls. It results in seeing women as inferiors, not just weaker physically but, without education, also less intelligent.

"Power over Others" Is Patriarchy

Patriarchy is a social-political system based on power, in which there is a hierarchy. The man at the top is alpha to those below, whether as head of a government, army, corporation, group of any kind, or family. Those at the top have more of whatever is desirable. In democracies, free enterprise is a competitive game, which is supposed to be regulated to curb unfair practices, but as we saw with the country's financial meltdown, greed and power manipulate "the game." The loss of livelihood, foreclosures on homes, and loss of medical insurance or tuition for college end dreams and possibilities for affected families. In social and business settings, in schoolyards and fraternities, having power over others can mean enjoying humiliating another person. Humiliation is often inflicted with deliberate intent, on someone perceived as an inferior. That person may then be filled with shame and suppressed rage, which fuels getting even, or when the humiliation is too great to bear, the victim may do a psychological sleight of hand, and later, will do to someone else what was done to him. This "identification with the aggressor" creates a culture of bullies in schoolyards, dysfunctional families, and dictatorships. Pervasive anxiety and paranoia are psychological consequences of this destructive pattern.

When men with status and power stick together, are not accountable for their behavior, and lack compassion, bad things happen. Gang rapes are done—in the 'hood, in conflicts by combatants, and on campuses by fraternity men. History professor Nicholas L. Syrett, author of *The Company He Keeps,* cites studies indicating that 70 to 90 percent of rapes on college campuses are committed by men in fraternities. Pedophilia in the Catholic Church endured for similar reasons—the lack of accountability in an elite group of entitled men. "Go along to get along" is a social pressure that boys learn early. The damage done can ruin lives, and reverberate down through generations. This is so for the humiliated and harmed victims, but also for the character and soul of the perpetrators—and those that remained silent. The use of power to dominate others or cover up abuses shifts greatly when there is gender balance. In this, as in many other situations, inclusion of women as equals in sufficient numbers to speak for feminine values opens the conversation and influences men who had remained silent to act from feelings and integrity.

Ever since the women's movement in the 1970s challenged rather than brought an end to gender stereotyping and limited gender roles, there have been major changes for women and men in the United States, especially in the middle class. It is no longer at all unusual to see women in positions of authority. However, the numbers relative to men are far from equal: In 2010, there were just 13 women CEOs of the 500 largest U.S. corporations. Congresswomen and women

senators held only 17 percent of the seats, with fewer coming to Washington in 2011. Women are called the empathic
gender, but not all women are. Men who take on nurturing
and caretaking roles in families and in professions develop
communication and empathic skills. As a result of the change
in cultural attitudes, it has become possible for many men
and women to develop a fuller range of skills and behaviors.
With these developmental changes, I would expect that brain
studies will show this and that this "Whole Person Brain"
will have the hemispheric symmetry of the Female Brain as
well as a larger corpus callosum joining them.

Taking Steps toward Saving the Planet and Ending Patriarchy

Maude Barlow, Canadian water activist and author of *Blue
Covenant,* is a spokesperson who sees the degradation of
women as a mirror of the degradation of the environment.
She sees patriarchal institutions such as the World Bank and
the World Water Council making anti-ecological decisions
as to who has access to water and who doesn't, based on seeing water as a profitable commodity and not as an integral
part of a living ecosystem, as a gift of nature. I like what she
has said to women about taking action:

> The biggest obstacle to action is the feeling that
> you're one little person and a woman at that, so what
> can you do? When you understand that every action
> matters, every single thing matters, change becomes
> possible. When we take an action, we are not alone,
> and we need to trust that millions of other people are

taking actions around the world, that we're making an impact. Maybe you stop drinking bottled water, or retrofit your house, or write to your member of parliament to say water is a human right—every act you take matters (*World Pulse*, 2010, p. 27).

I think that activism is about integrity and trust—a consistency, staying true to what you believe in small acts that no one sees, or big public ones, while at the same time believing that you are not alone and that there are others who feel and act as you do. This is where online connections help if in your own neighborhood, you are a seen as a kook or discounted. Each action is a choice that contributes toward a critical mass in bringing about change in collective thinking. This is how morphic fields work, the principle behind the allegory of the "Hundredth Monkey" or "Millionth Circle" as well as reaching a tipping point through geometric progression, the "3 to the 19th power" that explains how an infectious idea can spread like a virus once it reaches critical mass. Bear in mind that there is often little to indicate that what you are doing as an activist is having any effect—until critical mass is reached.

Chinese Bamboo Metaphor

There is another example that encourages those of us who have a sense of movement in the grassroots, who "feel" the energy field before the dream materializes. In my advocacy of a UN NGO World Conference on Women and Girls as a means toward gender equity and feminine values, I believe that the Chinese bamboo metaphor fits the situation. This is one of Olivier Clerc's metaphors in *Invaluable Lessons from a Frog: Seven Life-Enhancing Metaphors*: It is said that there is a very special variety of bamboo in China. If you sow seeds of this type on fertile ground, you have to be very patient. Nothing happens for years; there are no green shoots or any sign at all for the first, second, third, or fourth year. The fifth year, something green pushes through the soil, and then it grows forty feet in one year! The reason is simple, for years nothing happens on the surface, but the bamboo is developing prodigious roots until it is ready to manifest in the world. This is what bottom-up grassroots change looks like when a critical mass is reached. Suddenly, there is support, a new attitude, a confluence of effort and energy, and if enlightened leadership also manifests, a major cultural shift can happen.

Activism is an antidote against despair; whatever you do consciously to make a difference is doing something. It is also an expression of hope, as Vaclav Havel, playwright and first post-Communist Czech president defined it: "Hope is an orientation of spirit, an orientation of the heart. It is not the certainty that something will turn out well, but the conviction that something makes sense, no matter how it turns out."

Gratitude and Humility

The root word for humiliation, *humus,* means "earth," and is also the derivation of humility. In both, a person is humbled, but there is a world of difference between humiliation and humility. We are humbled when we are awed by a shift in perception, when the mystic in us perceives being in a loving universe, or part of something eternal, ancient, and divine, or realizes the gift of undeserved and unconditional love, or is moved by generosity that can never be repaid. Gratitude results.

I think back to my own experience of being deeply humbled, which changed my life. I was in high school and had gone with my close friend, Kay Hensley, to Forest Home, a Presbyterian camp in the mountains. It was the summer before my senior year and I was full of myself—popular, student body officer, academic and national debate honors. I was a star in my small world. One evening in the mountains, I listened to a talk that led to the realization that everything I had been so proud of, or considered my achievements, was not really of my doing. I thought of my impaired younger brother, Stephen, who having been disabled from birth would never even talk and whose ultimate fate in this life was to die in an institution. I realized in a moment of insight that I could have been him, that "there but for the grace of God, go I." While my perspective on divinity was self-centered in that moment, it did serve the higher purpose of deep gratitude. I thought that everything I had previously claimed as my accomplishments was actually the result of what I had been given: my parents, intelligence, talents, personality, and opportunities. I was humbled by and grateful for this realization. That evening, as I walked outside, the foremost question in my mind was "How do I say thank-you?" I went to the chapel and, in prayer, the realization came that the only way to express this would be to do for less-fortunate others, and the decision followed that it would be through being a doctor.

Since then, I've learned that there are many doctors, therapists, and nurses who are the healthy sibling in a family with an impaired child, possibly disproportionately so. I can understand that achievement is a way to get attention when so much is focused on the impaired sibling, or that the spared child achieves for the sibling as well. As often noted, there are multi-determinants why we turn out the way we do. Of all of them, for me being humbled, grateful, and motivated to say thank-you shaped my life and still does.

I wonder if this would have happened if I had not been in the mountains among the trees. This is from the perspective of being a tree person, which not everyone is. But because I am archetypally an Artemis, whose terrain is forest and mountain, being there I would be where my soul is at home, and I was receptive especially at night to mystical realms of meaning and connections. This archetype was also what drew me to Hildegard of Bingen, whose perspective and theology of *viriditas,* or "greening power," I naturally gravitated toward.

Hildegard made up the word *viriditas,* to mean the "greening power" of creation and creativity. Viriditas "is God's freshness that humans receive in their spiritual and physical life forces. It is the power of springtime, a germinating force, a fruitfulness that comes from God and permeates all creation. This powerful life force is found in the non-human as well the human" (Fox, *Illuminations of Hildegard of Bingen,* 1985, p. 32). Hildegard saw the divine in all creation through the greenness of the trees and beauty around her, which inspired her theology and art.

Hildegard of Bingen

Matthew Fox was a Dominican priest and scholar, author of *Original Blessings,* and founder of creation-centered theology

when he wrote the text for *Illuminations of Hildegard of Bingen*.
Hildegard of Bingen (1098–1179) was a remarkable woman
and not just for her time; her visions and voice reach us now
with great relevancy. She had a long and extraordinarily pro-
ductive and influential life. She was an abbess who created a
community of sisters independent of the local monastery and
over the objections of its abbot. She could have been called a
feminist, if the word had existed then. Hildegard was a mystic,
scholar, physician, botanist, artist, and musician. She left us
over seventy poems, seventy-two songs, and an opera; more
than one hundred letters written to emperors and popes, bish-
ops, archbishops, nuns, and nobility—she was an activist in
her time through her letters; and nine books, including three
major theological works: one on physiology; one on health;
and another on botanical, biological, and pharmacological
observations. She interpreted the Rule of Saint Benedict and
wrote commentaries on the gospels and saints. Her twenty-
five illuminations and commentaries on them have a range of
depth, symbology, and complexity.

I find in Hildegard's words and paintings an extraordinary resonance with the concerns and insights that motivated me to write this book. Her words of warning eight
hundred years ago are even more relevant today: "All nature
is at the disposal of humankind. We are to work with it.
Without it we cannot survive" (Fox, *Illuminations*, 1985,
p. 16). I marvel at her ecological spirituality and symbolic
consciousness, how she makes a connection between the
physical world and the sacred through symbols. I now can
appreciate the remarkably deep kinship between the origins
of Jungian analytic psychology in C. G. Jung's encounter with
the unconscious, which became fully known in 2009 with

the publication of *The Red Book,* fifty years after his death. Hildegard and Jung's paintings often began with a vision. I paid special attention when tree symbols appeared in their mandalas and paintings.

Hildegard's "Cultivating the Cosmic Tree" Mandala

This a beautiful cosmic wheel in which trees in their yearly seasons are tended by humans, representing the seasons of our lives from childhood to old age and death. Her trees have roots, trunk, and foliage, depending on the season. Drawing from her description of the vision and the meaning of it, Matthew Fox, in his discussion, wrote: "What Hildegard envisions in this mandala is the great work of humanity and creation cooperating; body and soul, water and Earth come together to bear fruit. For Hildegard, the cosmic tree and the world axis do not just sit there. They require cultivation and human creativity. The world is organic, but human ingenuity is required to bring the organism to its full potential" (Fox, *Illuminations,* 1985, p. 48).

Hildegard and Mysticism

Hildegard was an exceptional woman, especially for the times in which she lived. Her innate gifts that she was able to develop and practice, included leadership, intelligence, ability to express herself in words, painting, music, and *mysticism.* Mysticism is usually not described as a gift or talent—which some people have more inclinations toward than others, to develop further or not. I think of a mystic talent as similar in some ways to having an ear for music, perfect pitch, or seeing shades and nuances of color.

Mystic perception for Hildegard and many others is evoked in nature, by its beauty, its diversity, the sudden shifts of light and color, or by the sound or surprise at encountering another species, especially when this is a synchronicity, an encounter with a dream image, or important symbol, now in reality. Seeing a snake on your path can be startling, but when you have had a significant dream of a snake, it inspires awe and further reflection on the meaning of the dream. The sight of an eagle circling overhead easily catches your attention, but if this is your spirit animal from a guided meditation, dream, or shamanic journey, there is a similar sense of overlap or interpenetration between real world and inner world, which is a mystical experience. The sudden appearance of a large blue heron, with its iridescent coloration, in the midst of a significant conversation might feel like a shared special moment to two friends, but when the friends are both Jungian analysts, as happened with me, and we know that the iridescent shimmer appears in dreams where there is a connection with soul, it takes on a deeper significance. Where else, but in nature, are we so likely to be in the present moment and moved or awed by the wildness and sense of immensity around us? Nature also grounds and shields the mystic from materialists, for whom the invisible, interconnected, and divine world is nonsense.

Hildegard and the Artemis Archetype

Hildegard was born in a town on the Nahe River, which flows into the Rhine at Bingen, and lived her whole life in the lush green Rhineland valley. Here the Celts had once settled and, much as in Ireland, Celtic spirituality influences a mystical connection between land and people.

The Rhine valley was a perfect place for Hildegard to be born, raised, and then live in an abbey, where both the mystical and the many aspects of her intelligence could develop, and have the support of a community of sisters. It could be said that she shares the Artemis archetype with women as well as men who have a mystical connection to trees, forests, mountains, and glades, and who are protective of what they love, such as Greenpeace activists, the original women tree huggers, and Julia Butterfly Hill up in the tree she named "Luna." Artemis can be fierce or tender, like a mother bear looking after her cubs, which are helpless when young. Another quality of Artemis is a talent for disappearing like a deer into the forest—finding reasons to be out of doors, away from routine and people. One expression of Artemis as a goddess of the moon is as a mystic. To see by moonlight, which shifts from waxing to full and then waning into the dark of the moon, is an ability to be attuned to the atmosphere, to feel intuitively, and to be drawn instinctively toward what may be sensed, before it is seen clearly. Moonlight invites taking an "in breath" and being in a state of "Presence" and stillness, which is the realm of soul. Moonlight bathes the world we see in mystery; it is mystical light. In contrast, everyday reality is sunlight vision; we only see what is objectively visible. What is seen by sunlight would be the "ten thousand things" or physical manifestations of the underlying Onenenss or Tao, which corresponds to the Great Mystery among indigenous peoples.

Hildegard Country

I visited Hildegard's abbey in the Rhine Valley on a one-day trip on the German autobahn from the Netherlands where the trip began. A Dutch woman offered to take me to Bingen when I realized how close it was to where we were. I followed the map as she drove. On the west side of the Rhine over the town of Bingen, there was an elevation marked on the map as Mt. Druid. This was my first intimation of the Celtic connection between Ireland and Hildegard. We were now in the green and lush Rhineland country that had inspired Hildegard's *viriditas*. We crossed the river and drove up the narrow road through the fields around the abbey. It just began to rain when we arrived, which made us dash for shelter, first through the gate in the wall around the abbey and then into the building itself. We had entered a sacred space filled with the sweet sounds of women's voices singing the service. They were cloistered, and couldn't be seen. It was a sudden and welcome shift. The pressured high-speed drive down the autobahn and the search to find our destination was over. In this abbey on this rainy afternoon, I was in Hildegard country.

At that moment, "Hildegard country" was more than a place in the Rhine Valley. It was where my soul was— happy to be there, full of vitality and gratitude, in the present moment, with a glad-to-be-alive joyfulness, and an awareness of this moment of beauty and serenity. It's partaking in Hildegard's concept of *viriditas*, feeling full of the "greening power of springtime," which is to feel alive and blessed. One can be anywhere in the world and be in Hildegard country. Most recently, when I hiked through the aspens and pines, past meadows filled with wildflowers, to get to Oh Be Joyful waterfalls outside of Crested Butte, Colorado, I was once again in Hildegard country—it is a state of soul, it is to feel young and alive in nature, at any age. Local lore has it that James Cameron, who created the Na'vi world of Pandora for the film *Avatar*, was inspired by being in this high country of Colorado, which is the wildflower center of the state. It was easy to believe this, especially a day later when I was walking through waist-high, gorgeous, multi-hued, and delicate columbine flowers in a woodland of aspens. Nature's beauty helps, for sure, but to be in Hildegard country is more; it is to feel joy, to know that this moment is a divine gift. Whoever named the waterfall must have had similar feelings.

Gratitude and Service

I find that there are many people for whom gratitude leads to service, a desire to give to others out of the bountifulness of their lives. Taking privileges for granted is what we do until we learn how lucky we are, perhaps especially if of the female gender where vision sometimes doesn't extend very far beyond doing for the family and there may be little connection to others who are much less fortunate. The link between gratitude and service seems to be made more often and easily by people who realize that they are survivors, who don't take being alive or healthy or safe for granted and want to help others. Being privileged, unfortunately, often leads to feeling entitled, until the premise that to whom much has been given much is expected takes root. At the Peace Summit Conference in 2009 in Vancouver, Canada, the Dalai Lama said, "The world will be saved by Western women." This comment startled many people, but for many conscious and privileged Western women, it was a call to action.

Muir Woods

When I leave my house to drive over the hill and down to Muir Woods, I am going to Hildegard country. As I cross my entry deck, I can see the stump of the Monterey pine when I look for it. Other plants and branches have grown up around it and it blends in now with its surroundings. Maybe when this book is published, I will have it sanded to see the rings and the shape on what will then resemble a beautiful tabletop. Since I was at the United Nations when the tree was cut down, these two events and symbols are connected in my mind.

I am also reminded of the United Nations when I am in Muir Woods and take one of the paths through Cathedral Grove. There is a placard with photographs that reads:

> In 1945, delegates from all over the world met in San Francisco to establish the United Nations. On May 19, they traveled to Muir Woods to honor the memory of President Franklin Delano Roosevelt, whose death one month earlier had thrown the world into mourning. President Roosevelt believed in the value of national parks as sources of inspiration and human renewal. He also believed that good forestry practices and sustainable development of national resources were keystones to lasting peace around the world. Organizers of the event hoped that the profound beauty and serenity of Muir Woods would inspire delegates to pursue the president's program for world peace as they met to establish the United Nations.

Harold Ickes, the U.S. Secretary of the Interior in 1945, expressed his hope that the trees would be a positive influence on the delegates: "Here in such a 'temple of peace' the delegates would gain a perspective and sense of time that could be obtained nowhere else in America better than in such a forest. Muir Woods is a cathedral, the pillars of which have stood through much of recorded human history."

My Assignment

My daily walk through these redwoods began as exercise and became a walking meditation. There are places where I make a prayer stop. I've prayed for help with my assignment as message carrier and advocate for a United Nations 5th World Conference on Women as a means to reach a tipping point for women. It was a quixotic task, especially during the Bush administration years. A new fresh breeze of hope for women came into the United Nations with President Obama's appointments of Susan Rice as UN ambassador and an American delegation to the Commission on the Status of Women headed by Melanne Verveer, the first U.S. Ambassador on Women's Issues, a position created by Secretary of State Hillary Clinton.

Then in July 2010, the Gender Equality Architecture Reform (GEAR) campaign became successful, when the General Assembly voted unanimously to authorize and fund a new women's super-agency called UN Women to be headed by an under-secretary-general. The campaign was a four-year effort by over three hundred NGOs, with Charlotte Bunch and Bani Dugal as the spokeswomen. I envisioned Michelle Bachelet at the helm bringing about the UN 5th World Conference on Women (5WCW). She was the only one of twenty-five candidates nominated, with international stature as former president of Chile and a pediatrician, single mother, liberal, imprisoned by Pinochet, who left office at the end of her term with an 84 percent approval.

UN Women, as the sponsor of 5WCW with Michelle Bachelet, could create a conference that would bring women's issues and solutions to the attention of the world. It would be the impetus for women's circles to form all over the planet, leading to the metaphoric millionth circle or tipping point that ends patriarchy. Then masculine and feminine qualities could both be valued, and men and women could become equally empowered. This would be the first UN 5WCW supported by twenty-first century communication technology, which is capable of reaching cities and villages in all of the 192 countries that belong to the UN. The symbolic and logical year for it would be 2015. And, it makes sense to me that it might be held in New Delhi, India, since India is the largest democracy in the world and, at the same time, it is a third world country where so much progress is needed to make women's rights and human rights synonymous.

I wondered, "How do I get my message to Michelle Bachelet?" Then a synchronicity! My friend and sister-circle member, Isabel Allende, was leaving for Chile to accept Chile's highest literary award. She would have the opportunity to give president Bachelet a short letter from me, which she translated, and *Mensaje a las Mujeres* (the Spanish translation of *Urgent Message from Mother*)! While she was flying to Chile, UN Secretary-General Ban Ki-moon announced Bachelet's appointment. The next day Isabel had a ten-minute private conversation to speak for UN Women and 5WCW and to give her the book. The day after that, Bachelet was on her way to New York City—I hoped she brought it along as airplane reading. But whether or not, the timing of the conversation was uncanny, and there could be no better or persuasive a carrier of the message than Isabel Allende. It felt like a synchronicity. Time will tell.

Parting Thoughts

As I write the last chapter of this book, I'm aware and appreciative of the reader who had to follow a spiral path of thought, information, feelings, and images, from objective information to the subjective, intuitive, and mystical. I circumambulated around Tree, in the spirit of Jung's phrase "circumambulation of the Self." Tree was the *axis mundi* of this book, around which I wrote about what trees are, what they do, and what they symbolize and mean to us. To read to the end was to enter deeper into the forest of my experience and thoughts about trees, about patriarchy, women and girls, gnosis and soul. Always, always what concerns me most is meaning—what is the meaning of this reading experience? I hope memories and connections came to you as you read my words, and that the realization that you are a tree person will turn out to be very significant. What does it mean to be a tree person at this time in history? Might it have to do with participating in the next evolutionary step for humanity? Might it have to do with becoming a heart-inspired activist, when it matters?

We are on the edge of evolution or extinction. It calls upon those of us who are tree people to be spiritual activists, mystical activists, visionary activists, conscious activists, and sacred-feminine feminists. There is a necessity for equality between men and women in order for qualities that are now stereotyped as masculine and feminine to be developed in everyone, and for physiological gender differences to then complement or balance each other. Simple priorities: the children of the planet matter, everyone's children. The trees matter. Nothing on this planet is actually, really separate. Everything participates in the Tao or Great Mystery. The Eastern mystics and the indigenous people of the world know this.

I've been a passionate activist when a specific injustice or certainty stirs me to take a stand and sometimes to take a hit for doing so. I'm a private mystic—trusting the intuitive connection that keeps me in touch with soul and Self. I sense that activism and spirituality tap into an energy source, a morphic field (I feel it to be the *anima mundi*) that supports what we do out of love for the planet and those we share it with.

Andrew Harvey is calling on mystics to become activists. He has been a passionate mystic for whom the spiritual quest has been compelling. A brilliant young graduate of Oxford University, recognized and honored by being named a Fellow of All Souls College at twenty-one, he abandoned academic life to go on a spiritual quest that shaped his life and his teaching and writing. He was the subject of a 1993 BBC documentary, *The Making of a Modern Mystic*. His position, from the mystic end of the spectrum, in a nutshell:

The future of the planet hinges not on mysticism alone, nor on activism alone, but on the inspired marriage of these two potent forces. . . . Private pursuit of spiritual experience is absolutely not enough when the world is burning to death. It is absolutely incumbent on every single human being—including the ones who see the light in the trees—to do something real about the real problems in the real world. It is not spiritual to hide from them in a cloud of bliss. The detached transcendent spiritual ideal which reveals that world as an illusion is not true, because the world is not an illusion. That is bad mysticism (Church and Gendreau, *Healing Our Planet*, 2005, p. 104).

I believe that the feminine principle and sacred feminine are coming into consciousness through women and men, and that once women hold up half the sky and men take care of half the Earth, a sacred balance between masculine and feminine becomes possible, and a new evolutionary step is taken. Emergence of the sacred feminine is about immanence, the sacredness in matter. She heals the split between body and soul in the individual, and when brought fully into collective consciousness will restore to Earth the *anima mundi* or soul of the world.

The feminine is not hierarchal, does not see in black and white, or consider options as either-or. Look around us at what Mother Nature has created for the best and most flamboyant expression of the Feminine. The feminine celebrates diversity, individuality, creativity, colors, forms, sounds, is seemingly disorderly and yet functional. To learn about what goes on in one tree is an awesome lesson in collaboration and interdependency. These are qualities that women have access to when they work out solutions in circles, and draw from experience. This is also how men work together as a team, when freed of alpha-male ego needs for hierarchy. To be like a tree is non-patriarchal; for a tree, everything to do with surviving, thriving, and growing is interconnected. What happens within a tree or between trees or with life around the trees is not based on theory or theology or the right to take more.

In her speech "Come September" at the Lannan Foundation in Santa Fe, New Mexico, in September 2002, author Arundhati Roy spoke of the global context in which the two towers of the World Trade Center were destroyed on September 11, 2001. It was a historical tour de force about the toll in suffering and conflicts caused by efforts to control the world. Then, at the very end, her words took the listener from the state of the world as we know it to the one that could be coming: "Another world is not only possible, she is on her way. Maybe many of us won't be here to greet her, but on a quiet day, if I listen very carefully, I can hear her breathing."

This is, of course, the hope: that there is enough time for trees and tree people to save our beautiful planet from turning into a wasteland, and heal the wounds of patriarchy with its focus on dominance over everything. It is this dominator mentality that separates us from each other, from all other species, and makes it impossible to have soul connections or sense them. We are in a period of crisis—where danger and opportunity exist side by side. The situation calls for intelligence, mysticism, wisdom, and compassion to find ways we can act individually and together to save the planet and restore soul. Whatever comes to your mind and heart, as an intention or a dream, take the first step that has its origins in who you are and what has meaning for you. The path will open up as you travel it. There will be companions.

With love and hope,
Jean Shinoda Bolen, MD

DISCUSSION/REFLECTION
QUESTIONS

I suggest that a discussion group be held in a circle with something symbolic in the center. It is my hope that *Like a Tree* will lead readers to recollect and share their experiences, think more deeply into many subjects, conclude that it matters what we do, individually and collectively, and go from there. These questions are for the individual reader as well.

Introduction: Like a Tree. On being a tree person or a not-tree person: Did you immediately identify yourself as one or the other? Childhood recollections? Is there a particular tree or trees that you would try to save or would mourn?

Chapter 1. Standing Like a Tree. An introduction to what an individual tree is and does (anatomy, physiology, ecosystems, types), what tropical rain forests and boreal rain forests are, what they do and efforts to save them, and an appreciation of ancient trees. This is information that can evoke wonder. Did you learn something about trees that touched your heart? This question leads to Activism with Heart. Here the most important idea is how to recognize "an assignment" or a cause that is yours: Is this meaningful? Will it be fun? (Fun has to do with who the people are and being able to draw on your talents and creativity.) Is it motivated by love?

Chapter 2. Giving Like a Tree. Insights into how trees created and continue to provide what we need for life and that "Mother Earth" provides for us much in the same way that the physiology of our personal mother did when she was pregnant and we were inside her. There is a need to realize that trees and the planet are our "Giving Tree," and that the relationship between the boy and the tree in the children's book *The Giving Tree* applies to us, with the fate of Easter Island a lesson on what not to do. Discuss the premise that "not enough trees, too many people" is one cause of global warming; this brings in the subject of reproductive rights and limits on population growth. Might reforestation and reproductive rights go hand in hand?

Chapter 3. Surviving Like a Tree. About how trees and women are devalued and treated like exploitable property and how trees and women are needed to save the planet. What is your reaction to being called a "tree hugger"? What is the actual history—the Chipko movement? Do you relate to Artemis as goddess and archetype: is she an aspect of you? Thoughts about Betty Makoni, Julia Butterfly Hill, *Avatar* the movie? Is gender equality necessary to save the planet?

Chapter 4. Sacred Like a Tree. People who perceive trees or sites as sacred differ from those who do not. Might this be a characteristic of a tree person, or only of some tree people? After reading Bolen's definition of "Aphrodite consciousness," does this fit with your own experience? Any thoughts about the unusual founding of Findhorn, or Allen Meredith and yew trees? Might you heed such a voice?

Chapter 5. Symbolic Like a Tree. Trees have been mythic, archetypal, religious, cosmic, and personal symbols. It would be of value to take a few minutes in silence to invite images and memories of trees to come to mind. Real and remembered trees, photographs, or paintings—or totally new images—may come. Discuss these images and associations. Discuss reactions to the familiar story of the expulsion from the Garden of Eden as drawn from scholarship and psychology. Does this lead you to reinterpret the story? This story is the basis on which the sin of Eve is placed upon women in Judeo-Christian-Islamic religions.

Chapter 6. Soulful Like a Tree. This chapter invites readers to remember soulful moments. Begin with the question: How is a tree soulful? For people who are psychologically minded: why did Siddhartha set out on his quest? For spiritual inquiry: what is enlightenment? With Bolen's broad definition of a bodhisattva, who that you know qualifies?

Chapter 7. Wise Like a Tree: Tree People. Trees are the heart of ecosystems and the lungs of the Earth; they have adapted, are giving, diverse, and interdependent, and have many similarities to how women function and are treated. What is your response to the following quote?

> "Another world is not only possible, she is on her way. Maybe many of us won't be here to greet her, but on a quiet day, if I listen very carefully, I can hear her breathing."

RESOURCES

Books

Amnesty International. *Stop Violence Against Women: It's in Our Hands*. London: Amnesty International Publications, 2005.

Barstow, Anne Lewellyn. *Witchcraze: A New History of the European Witch Hunts, 1560–1760*. London: Pandora, 1995.

Bolen, Jean Shinoda. *Close to the Bone: Life-Threatening Illness as a Soul Journey*. New York: Scribner, 1996; rev. ed., Berkeley, CA: Conari Press, 2007.

———. *Crossing to Avalon*. San Francisco, CA: HarperCollins, 1994; "The Greening of the Wasteland: Findhorn," pp. 207–25.

———. *Goddesses in Everywoman*. San Francisco, CA: Harper & Row, 1984; New York: Harper Collins, 2004; "Artemis," pp. 46–73; "Athena," pp. 75–106; "The Alchemical Goddess," pp. 224–32; "Aphrodite," pp. 233–262.

———. *The Millionth Circle: How to Change Ourselves and The World*. Berkeley, CA: Conari Press, 1999.

———. *Ring of Power*. San Francisco, CA: HarperSanFrancisco, 1992; York Beach, ME: Nicolas-Hays, 1999.

———. *The Tao of Psychology: Synchronicity and the Self*. New York: HarperCollins, 1979, 2004.

———. *Urgent Message from Mother: Gather the Women, Save the World*. San Francisco, CA: Conari Press, 2005.

Brizendine, Louann. *The Female Brain*. New York: Broadway Books, 2005.

———. *The Male Brain*. New York: Broadway Books, 2010.

Caldecott, Moyra. *Myths of the Sacred Tree*. Rochester, VT: Destiny Books, 1993.

Charpentier, Louis. *The Mysteries of Chartres Cathedral*. London: Research into Lost Knowledge Organisation Trust, 1997.

Chetan, Anand, and Diana Brueton. *The Sacred Yew: Rediscovering the Ancient "Tree of Life" Through the Work of Allen Meredith*. London: Arkana, 1994.

Church, Dawson, and Geralyn Gendreau (eds.). *Healing Our Planet: Healing Our Selves*. Santa Rosa, CA: Elite Books, 2005; particularly the chapters by Andrew Harvey, "Mystical Activism," and Alberto Villoldo, "Homo Luminous: New Shamans of the West."

Clerc, Olivier. *Invaluable Lessons from a Frog: Seven Life-Enhancing Metaphors*. Flourtown, PA: Dreamriver Press, 2009.

Collis, John Stewart. *The Triumph of the Tree*. New York: Sloane, 1954.

Cowan, James G. *Letters from a Wild State: Rediscovering Our True Relationship to Nature*. New York: Belltower, 1991.

Davies, Steve. "The Canaanite-Hebrew Goddess." *The Book of the Goddess, Past and Present*. Ed. Carl Olson. New York: Crossroad, 1985.

Diamond, Jared. *Collapse: How Societies Choose to Fail or Succeed*. New York: Viking, 2005.

Dunning, Joan, with photographs by Doug Thron. *From the Redwood Forest: Ancient Trees and the Bottom Line: A Headwaters Journey.* White River Junction, VT: Chelsea Green, 1998.

Dworkin, Andrea. *Woman Hating: A Radical Look at Sexuality.* New York: Feminist Press, 1973.

Fox, Matthew. *Illuminations of Hildegard of Bingen.* Text by Hildegard of Bingen with commentary by Matthew Fox. Santa Fe, NM: Bear & Co., 1985.

———. *Original Blessing: A Primer in Creation Spirituality Presented in Four Paths, Twenty-Six Themes, and Two Questions.* New York: Jeremy P. Tarcher/Putnam, 1983.

Franck, Frederick. *The Zen of Seeing: Seeing/Drawing as Meditation.* New York: Random House, 1973.

Frazer, James George. *The New Golden Bough: A New Abridgment of the Classic Work,* edited and with notes and foreword by Theodore H. Gaster. New York: Criterion Books, 1959.

Gendler, J. Ruth. *Notes on the Need for Beauty: An Intimate Look at an Essential Quality.* New York: Marlowe, 2007.

Gore, Al. *Our Choice: A Plan to Solve the Climate Crisis.* Emmaus, PA: Rodale Books, 2009.

———. *An Inconvenient Truth: The Planetary Emergency of Global Warming and What We Can Do about It.* Emmaus, PA: Rodale, 2006.

Graves, Robert. *The White Goddess.* New York: Farrar, Straus & Giroux, 1966.

Hill, Julia Butterfly. *The Legacy of Luna: The Story of a Tree, a Woman, and the Struggle to Save the Redwoods.* San Francisco, CA: HarperSanFrancisco, 2000.

Jung, C. G. "Confrontation with the Unconscious." *Memories, Dreams, Reflections.* New York: Pantheon Books, 1963.

———. "The Philosophical Tree" (1934). In *The Collected Works of C. G. Jung,* Vol. 13, *Alchemical Studies,* Bollingen Series XX, trans. R. F. C. Hull. Princeton, NJ: Princeton University Press, 1967.

———. *The Red Book.* New York: W. W. Norton, 2009.

Kerenyi, Carl. *Eleusis: Archetypal Image of Mother and Daughter,* trans. Ralph Manheim. New York: Bollingen Foundation/ Pantheon Books, 1967.

Kristof, Nicholas D., and Sheryl WuDunn. *Half the Sky: Turning Oppression into Opportunity for Women Worldwide.* New York: Alfred A. Knopf, 2009.

LeClaire, Anne D. *Listening Below the Noise: A Meditation on the Practice of Silence.* New York: HarperCollins, 2009.

Lewington, Anna, and Edward Parker. *Ancient Trees: Trees That Live for a Thousand Years.* London: Collins and Brown, 1999.

Louv, Richard. *Last Child in the Woods: Saving Our Children from Nature-Deficit Disorder.* Chapel Hill, NC: Algonquin Books of Chapel Hill, 2008.

Lyons, Dana. *The Tree.* Bellevue, WA: Illumination Arts Publishing, 2002.

Maclean, Dorothy. *Call of the Trees.* Issaquah, WA: Lorian Association, 2006.

Mehdi, Sharon. *The Great Silent Grandmother Gathering: A Story for Anyone Who Thinks She Can't Save the World.* New York: Viking, 2005.

Melton, Patricia Smith (editor and photographer). *Sixty Years, Sixty Voices: Israeli and Palestinian Women.* Washington, DC: PeaceXPeace; *www.peacexpeace.org.*

Metzger, Deena, *The Woman Who Slept with Men to Take the War Out of Them & Tree: Two Works in One Volume.* Culver City, CA: Peace Press, 1981.

Muir, John. *My First Summer in the Sierra*. New York: Houghton Mifflin, 1911.

Neihardt, John G. *Black Elk Speaks: Being the Life Story of a Holy Man of the Oglala Sioux*. Lincoln: University of Nebraska Press, 1961.

Nhat Hanh, Thich. "The Last Tree." In Allan Hunt Badiner (ed.). *Dharma Gaia: A Harvest of Essays in Buddhism and Ecology*. Berkeley, CA: Parallax Press, 1990.

Pakenham, Thomas. *Meetings with Remarkable Trees*. New York: Random House, 1998.

——— . *Remarkable Trees of the World*. New York: W. W. Norton, 2002.

Sheldrake, Rupert, *The Rebirth of Nature: The Greening of Science and God*. Rochester, VT: Park Street Press, 1994.

Silverstein, Shel. *The Giving Tree*. New York, HarperCollins, 1992.

Suzuki, David, and Wayne Grady. *Tree: A Life Story*. Berkeley, CA: Greystone Books, 2004.

Syrett, Nicholas L. *The Company He Keeps: A History of White College Fraternities*. Chapel Hill: University of North Carolina Press, 2009.

Taylor, Bron. *Dark Green Religion: Nature Spirituality and the Planetary Future*. Berkeley, CA: University of California Press, 2010.

Totman, Conrad. *The Green Archipelago: Forestry in Preindustrial Japan*. Athens, OH: Ohio University Press, 1998.

TreePeople, with Andy and Katie Lipkis. *The Simple Act of Planting a Tree: A Citizen Forester's Guide to Healing Your Neighborhood, Your City, and Your World*. Los Angeles, CA: Tarcher, 1990.

Tudge, Colin. *The Tree: A Natural History of What Trees Are, How They Live, and Why They Matter*. New York: Crown, 2006.

Articles/Publications

Adams, William Lee. "Rebecca Hosking: Banning Plastic Bags." *Time*, September 21, 2009, p. 52.

Barton, Adriana. "Eco-Spirituality: Perhaps the Vatican Should Be Worried about Nature Worship." *Globe and Mail*, January 25, 2010.

Beeler, Meg. "Connecting with the Web," *Shifting Consciousness News*, August 2006, *www.earthcaretakers.net*

"Charlie Toledo Interview." Nature Speaks Project, *www .naturespeaks.org/toledo_charlie*, January 18, 2005.

Fox, Thomas C. "Vatican Investigates U.S. Women Religious Leadership." *National Catholic Reporter*, April 14, 2009; *ncronline.org/news/women/vatican-investigates-us-women-religious-leadership*

"Girls Count." Center for Global Development, International Center for Research on Women and Population Council, 2008; *www.cgdev.org/content/publications/detail/15154*

Goetz, Anne Marie (lead author). "Who Answers to Women?: Gender and Accountability." UNIFEM (United Nations Development Fund for Women) series, *Progress of the World's Women 2008–2009*; *www.unifem.org*

Greenpeace. "Slaughtering the Amazon," 2009 report.

Hari, Johann. "Can One Woman Save Africa?" [Wangari Maathai] *Independent*, September 28, 2009.

Kristof, Nicholas D. "Another Pill That Could Cause a Revolution." *The New York Times*, August 1, 2010.

Kristof, Nicholas D., and Sheryl WuDunn. "Why Women's Rights Are the Cause of Our Time." *New York Times Magazine*, August 23, 2009, pp. 28–51.

Madden, Kristen. "Passevara, the Sacred Earth." *Parabola*, Spring 1999.

McNeill, Barbara. "Edgar Mitchell: Cosmic Activist." *Shift* (magazine of the Institute of Noetic Sciences), Issue 12, November 2006.

"Meg Beeler Interview." Nature Speaks Project, *www.naturespeaks .org/beeler_meg*, January 12, 2008.

Montaigne, Fen. "The Great Northern Forest Boreal." *National Geographic 201*, June, 2002, pp. 42–65.

Nickens, T. Edward. "Paper Chase." *Audubon,* January–February 2009; *audubonmagazine.org/features0901/habitat.html.*

Smedley, Jenny. "Sacred World Series: Sacred Trees," August 2, 2005; *www.merliannews.com/artman/publish/article_512.shtml*

Staff article (not attributed). "Gendercide: The Worldwide War on Baby Girls." *Economist,* March 6–12, 2010, pp. 13, 77–80.

Taylor, S. E., L. C. Klein, B. P. Lewis, et al. "Female Responses to Stress: Tend and Befriend, Not Flight or Fight." *Psychological Review* 2000, pp. 411–29.

UNIFEM (United Nations Development Fund for Women). "UNIFEM 2008–2009 Annual Report." UNIFEM, 2009; *www.unifem.org*

UNIFEM/UNDP. "Making the MDGs [Millennium Development Goals] Work Better for Women: Implementing Gender-Responsive National Development Plans and Programmes." UNIFEM (United Nations Development Fund for Women)/ UNDP (United Nations Development Programme), 2009; *www.unifem.org/materials*

United Nations Girls Education Initiative. "Zimbabwe: Profile on Betty Makoni and the Girl Child Network, May 16, 2007; *www.ungei.org*

Wallace, Scott. "Last of the Amazon." *National Geographic,* January 2007.

Walton, John. "Tree Planting in the Driest Place on Earth." *BBC News Magazine,* April 20, 2009.

World Pulse: Global Issues through the Eyes of Women, Spring/ Summer 2010 (Edina Yahana, pp. 32–33; Maude Barlow, p. 27).

Websites

Advocacy for a UN 5th World Conference on Women: *www.5wcw.org.*

Arundhati Roy's speech "Come September" at the Lannan Foundation in Santa Fe, New Mexico, September 2002: archives at *www.lannan.org*

Berkeley Oak Grove Controversy: *en.wikipedia.org/wiki/Berkeley_oak_grove_controversy*

"Berkeley Treesitters and the Nature of Protest" (by Meta Ghost) *www.dailykos.com/story/2007/12/22/104859/51/199/422875*

Bodhi tree historical information: *www.buddhamind.info/leftside/arty/bod-leaf.htm*

Buddha Mind: *www.buddhamind.info*

Center for Global Development, International Center for Research on Women and Population Council: *www.cgdev.org*

"Declaration of Sentiments" Seneca Falls, 1848. US Constitution Online: *www.usconstitution.net/sentiments.html.*

Earth Caretakers: *www.earthcaretakers.net*

Earth Child Institute. *www.earthchildinstitute.org.*

Findhorn Foundation: *www.findhorn.org*

Garry Oaks: *www.for.gov.bc.ca/hfd/library/documents/treebook/garryoak.htm* and *en.wikipedia.org/wiki/Berkeley_oak_grove_controversy*

Greenpeace Kleercut campaign (2004–2009): *www.kleercut.net*

Institute of Noetic Sciences (IONS): *www.noetic.org*

Jean Shinoda Bolen. *www.jeanbolen.com.*

Lovelock Gaia hypothesis: *en.wikipedia.org/wiki/James_Lovelock*

National Geographic: *www.nationalgeographic.com/eye/ deforestation/effect.html*

Nature Speaks Project (Linda Milks): *www.naturespeaks.org*

TreePeople: *www.treepeople.org*

United Nations Development Fund for Women (UNIFEM): *www .unifem.org*

United Nations Girls' Education Initiative (UNGEI): *www.ungei .org/infobycountry/zimbabwe_1419.html* Zimbabwe. Betty Makoni and the Girl Child Network.

United Nations Women. *www.unwomen.org.*

Documentaries

Burns, Ken, and Dayton Duncan. *The National Parks: America's Best Idea.* Documentary distributed by PBS, 2009.

Cvitanovich, Frank. *The Making of a Modern Mystic.* BBC documentary on Andrew Harvey, 1993.

Disney, Abigail, and Gini Reticker. *Pray the Devil Back to Hell.* Women who brought peace to Liberia, 2008.

Read, Donna. *The Burning Times.* Part 2 of a series that includes *Goddess Remembered* and *Full Circle.* Canadian Film Board documentary, 1990. *www.nfb.ca/film/burning_times/free download.*

Risley, Michealene Cristini: *Tapestries of Hope.* Documentary about Betty Makoni, founder of Girl Child Network. *www .tapestriesofhope.com*

INDEX

ACKNOWLEDGMENTS

While I was writing this book, I walked almost daily in Muir Woods. I think of this forest as a support and muse for *Like a Tree*. This national park is a sanctuary of old growth redwood trees. It exists because of William Kent's (1864–1928) donation of land, the legislation he wrote as a congressman to establish the National Park Service, and the lobbying he did for a State Park system and Mount Tamalpais State Park. I am grateful to him and all of the others who established this and our other state and national parks.

My thanks to a grove of tree people for their support, the conveners of the Millionth Circle: to Betty Rothenberger, Clare Peterson, Judy Grosch, Betty Karr, Penny McManigal, Ann Smith, Katherine Collis, and Donna Goodman, who provided stories and information. To Anne Caldwell, Valerie Macfarland, Nancy Grandfield, Peggy Sebera, Justine Toms, Linda Merryman, Leslie Lanes, Andrea Wachter, Joy Adams, Onzie Stevens, Elly Pradervand, Rosemary Williams, Ronita Johnson, Joan

Kenley, and Elinore Detiger, ex-officio member, who held it in the incubation space of the circle.

To the sisters of perpetual disorder, my prayer circle of tree people for their visible and invisible help: Grace Damman, Carole Robinson, Toni Triest, Isabel Allende, and especially Pauline Tesler, who took the cover photograph of "author in tree" after many trees were climbed and many photographs were taken. To Monika Wikman for experiences that were incorporated into the book.

To Jan Johnson at Conari Press, for her early support for *Like a Tree,* and Katinka Matson, my agent at Brockman, tree people who related to the book from the beginning. To the people of Conari who turn a manuscript into a book, and the marketing and publicity staff, especially Bonni Hamilton, another tree person, who will help it reach an audience.

Thank you.

ABOUT THE AUTHOR

Jean Shinoda Bolen, M.D., is a psychiatrist, Jungian analyst, and an internationally known author and speaker who draws from spiritual, feminist, Jungian, medical, and personal wellsprings of experience. She is the author of *The Tao of Psychology, Goddesses in Everywoman, Gods in Everyman, Ring of Power, Crossing to Avalon, Close to the Bone, The Millionth Circle, Goddesses in Older Women, Crones Don't Whine, Urgent Message from Mother,* and *Like a Tree* She is a Distinguished Life Fellow of the American Psychiatric Association, and a former clinical professor of psychiatry at the University of California at San Francisco, and a past board member of the Ms. Foundation for Women and the International Transpersonal Association. She was a recipient of the Institute for Health and Healing's "Pioneers in Art, Science, and the Soul of Healing Award," and is a Diplomate of the American Board of Psychiatry and Neurology. She was in two acclaimed documentaries, the Academy-Award-winning anti-nuclear proliferation film *Women—For America, For the World,* and the Canadian Film Board's *Goddess Remembered.* Learn more at Jean's website, *www.jeanshinodabolen.com.*

TO OUR READERS

Mango Publishing, established in 2014, publishes an eclectic list of books by diverse authors—both new and established voices—on topics ranging from business, personal growth, women's empowerment, LGBTQ studies, health, and spirituality to history, popular culture, time management, decluttering, lifestyle, mental wellness, aging, and sustainable living. We were recently named 2019 and 2020's #1 fastest growing independent publisher by *Publishers Weekly*. Our success is driven by our main goal, which is to publish high quality books that will entertain readers as well as make a positive difference in their lives.

Our readers are our most important resource; we value your input, suggestions, and ideas. We'd love to hear from you—after all, we are publishing books for you!

Please stay in touch with us and follow us at:

Facebook: Mango Publishing
Twitter: @MangoPublishing
Instagram: @MangoPublishing
LinkedIn: Mango Publishing
Pinterest: Mango Publishing
Newsletter: mangopublishinggroup.com/newsletter

Join us on Mango's journey to reinvent publishing, one book at a time.